NEVER GIVE UP - THERE IS ALWAYS HOPE.

by Niall McHugo

Copyright @ 2023 Niall McHugo
ISBN: 9798373853293
All rights reserved.

Dedicated to my amazing children
Ava, Finn & Eli.
Love Daddy xxx

"Sport has the power to change the world...it has the power to inspire. It has the power to unite people in a way that little else does. It speaks to youth in a language they understand. Sport can create hope where once there was only despair."
- Nelson Mandela

About the Author

I am a primary school Principal from Virginia, Co. Cavan. I am 44 years old and I have three amazing children. Their names are Ava, Finn and Eli who are currently, 12, 10 and 6 months old. I played Gaelic football for twenty-five years in Cavan and one year in America. I was an extremely passionate player who gave everything for the sport that I loved to play. I battled hard to play and win something with my club but I came across various challenges that I had to overcome in life along the way. As bad as things became I never gave up.

I am currently The Health and Wellbeing Officer and club PRO for my local GAA club. Since retiring from football I have helped as a selector or manager of various teams from the U17's, Junior and the senior Ladies Team in my parish.

My purpose in writing this book is to make people aware that when they experience dark moods there is always someone who can help. It might be, like in my case, the support of those involved in sport, maybe a professional counsellor, maybe a friend, maybe a family member or a combination of all. I hope my story has shown that to be the case, and that life has many good, adventurous and even witty things to offer. It would be a pity to miss out on them and we can all experience them if we "Never Give Up"!

For those who know someone who is struggling, you can help by just being there for them and by remembering to "Never Give Up"!

While my story focuses on the support I found from my involvement in the GAA, I hope that what I learned generally will help anyone in a similar situation, whether involved in sport or not, that there is always someone or something that will keep you going.

This is my first book and I plan to write a second book next year.

Contents

Chapter 1:	Something Not Right	7
Chapter 2:	Telling the Family	15
Chapter 3:	Back to the Beginning	20
Chapter 4:	County Call Up	29
Chapter 5:	Winning Championships was Easy	34
Chapter 6:	Coming to America	43
Chapter 7:	Social Side of Football - The Pub	49
Chapter 8:	Oz and Back	54
Chapter 9:	Supersize Me	64
Chapter 10:	New Manager - New Hope	74
Chapter 11:	Decision Time	82
Chapter 12:	Fresh Beginnings	88
Chapter 13:	Timing is Key	96
Chapter 14:	The Road to Recovery	103
Chapter 15:	Was this the End?	106
Chapter 16:	Keeping Busy	111
Chapter 17:	New Season - New Me	114
Chapter 18:	Home	123
Chapter 19:	Life Without Football	129
Chapter 20:	One Life - One Club?	133
Chapter 21:	Tips to People to Help Understand	142
Chapter 22:	Nice Things to do for Yourself	152
Chapter 23:	Hope	161
Useful Contacts		167
Acknowledgement		171

"Darkness cannot drive out darkness; only light can do that. Hate cannot drive out hate; only love can do that." - Martin Luther King, Jr.

Chapter 1 - Something Not Right

I was starting to feel down in the dumps. I was in a constant haze. Even a bright summer's days seemed grey. Both of my two older children's birthdays came and went. I didn't feel a part of anything. I felt like a stranger in my own home. I didn't want to do anything or meet anyone. I was just 'happy' to stay home. I just couldn't snap out of it. I wasn't feeling myself at all. Every day just dragged and even a smile was becoming harder and harder to force. I was having dark thoughts, thoughts of things being better were I not around. I didn't feel I would be missed. I found myself spending more and more time in my bedroom alone. Tears came very easily. I was at the lowest point of my life. I thought of my beautiful children and I tried to snap out of these thoughts. These were thoughts that I would have previously deemed as very selfish and I never once dreamt I would be having them. I would distract myself and keep busy but as much as I tried, it didn't stop these horrible thoughts creeping slowly back into my mind. Any time my mind was still, even for a moment, these thoughts reappeared. It was like smoke finding a gap under a door, I couldn't fill the gap and stop it from seeping in. Sometimes I would lie in my bed staring at the ceiling with these dark images flowing freely through my mind. I was glad they were unwelcome thoughts as I never made plans but they were racing around in my head and I couldn't get them out. I had thoughts where I felt it would be easier not to be around anymore. Maybe the pain would finally go as I felt in such pain everyday from the minute I woke up to the minute going to bed. When I went very low it was a dark and scary place to be. I had no energy and there was no light getting in at all. I didn't want to see anyone and I started to think more of what it would be like if I wasn't around anymore. It is like you are in so much pain inside that your body is screaming at you to just end it. You often hear the analogy using dark clouds but it felt like a dark force pushing your shoulders down and smothering you slowly. All your positivity and spark is sucked out of your body and you feel like you are drowning in mud. Your voice is gone, your body is tired but your mind never stops racing. Every negative situation plays on repeat in your mind. You get more paranoid about people and make every good memory seem the opposite.

The only thing that really kept me from doing anything was the pain I would cause if I left. The pain left behind. I pictured my two eldest children dressed in black at my funeral, throwing a rose each on my coffin and both unsure of what to do whilst crying and looking so confused wondering why I left them. I can see my boy's face utterly devastated that I was gone but he was so afraid. My daughter just frozen. My little baby boy would be there oblivious but he would grow up without a Dad and I would never see his smile again. My partner, utterly devastated leaving her as a single mother rearing our son alone. My parents, utterly heartbroken and just not able to cope. I pictured my mother being supported at the funeral unable to walk with the heartbreak. My Dad, who rarely cries, unable to hold in the tears. My brother, sisters, nephews and nieces unable to stop crying whilst wondering WHY? The devastation left behind would be like me hurting someone on purpose. I could never hurt anyone so why would I hurt them now and disappear where they would never find answers. It would be such a severe punishment for everyone close to me. I had to find a way out of this blackness.

As time went on things didn't get any better. I started to pull away from people as I didn't want to be asked any questions or be seen. I even felt my face was starting to look grey in complexion and drained looking. The sparkle in my eyes had dulled. It was like the negativity was draining the colour from my body. I stopped visiting my parents and my siblings. My parents were trying to phone and send messages and were starting to worry but I couldn't face telling them. I couldn't tell them as I didn't know what was going on either. I wasn't sleeping very well, not eating much so I was losing weight and lacking energy. I had no appetite for food or life and felt everything in life was a struggle. Of course I would go into work everyday and be full of energy, the life and soul of the party, full of smiles but the reality was it was all a show. This is such a worry as sometimes it is the happiest of people who are hiding it all inside. It can be the person who looks like life is going perfectly. Someone who has a great job, a lovely family, captain of the football team or if you went by their social media they look like life is great. Sometimes these are the people who are struggling and putting on a show like I did. This is why it is so hard for family and friends to spot. Nobody knows what goes on behind closed doors and who is struggling. Thankfully a doctor's appointment was made for me.

As bad as I felt, even the thought of making a doctor's appointment was not on my radar but I was so glad a call was made and I was booked in. I began to think about how and what I would say. My plan was to chat to the doctor and to just come clean and I would tell them how bad everything was and that I felt I needed some kind of help. I would be very open for any suggestions and recommendations. The day finally came and I rehearsed what I would say. I arrived at the surgery and took my seat awaiting my name to be called on the tannoy. I hated the waiting room and the silence between coughs of sick people waiting to be seen. This waiting time was also slightly uncomfortable for me. When you walk into the waiting room, you would quickly glance for a free chair but also hoping not to see a familiar face. If you saw a person you know but not well enough to sit down beside I might give a nod and sit as far away as possible. The fear of instigating a conversation for all to hear would be more torture. As I got closer to the chairs I would try to avoid the old man or lady who hasn't seen anyone all day and is mad to chat. These are the ones who ask you why you are seeing the doctor! Then you have the crying toddler dripping snot on all the toys and magazines. So when I picked a seat it was really like picking the best of a bad lot, just hoping the wait wouldn't be too long. While waiting, you look around and wonder what is wrong with everyone and why they are seeing the doctor. The people coughing show their cards quickly. It's the quiet, healthy looking people that get you thinking. I am sure everyone waiting thinks the same. Finally, my name was called. Whew! I managed to avoid a conversation and I didn't see anyone I knew too well.

I walked into the doctor's room and I took a seat beside the pine desk. I started to tell the doctor in a kind of code that I was feeling low. I said I was very tired and I felt drained. I had planned to tell him loads of symptoms of depression and I hoped that he would work it out. I went on to mention that I had no appetite and I was not sleeping great. He nodded his head and he ran a few tests and he said that all seemed fine. I knew I was not fine but I was so afraid to say anything. I just couldn't bring myself to announce to him that I was feeling very low. I got up from my chair so disappointed with myself and I went to walk towards the door. I was now feeling worse inside as I couldn't say it. As I reached for the door handle, I was thrown a lifeline. "Is there anything else?", the doctor said. My heart stopped for a few seconds as I froze at the door. Then my heart skipped a beat and began to race. This was my chance I thought. I felt he knew by my eyes that they were crying out for help even though my mouth wouldn't open. I turned around, walked towards the black leather chair and I sat back down and began to cry. I think it was a mix of relief and my secret cry for help was finally spotted. I knew it was now the time to talk. He asked me some very sensitive questions and the tears continued as I tried to answer these as honestly as possible, as difficult as they were. The doctor was making notes but also making sure to show he cared. I will never forget the four words the doctor uttered while looking me in the eye. "You are clinically depressed." Hearing those words made me feel weak as I believed there was a stigma attached to depression in Ireland. While I was shocked with what the doctor had just said, as that term sounded serious, I was also so relieved as I now knew what was wrong with me. The doctor went on to explain that in my brain there was an imbalance of serotonin which was very common. He said that as many as 'one in three people' suffer from these imbalances. That's a good few lads in the football team I thought to myself or in every team for that matter. I thought of the starting XV of my team and said to myself that it means five lads on the starting team alone have this. Maybe I wasn't so abnormal after all.

I immediately felt more comfortable. "Serotonin levels influence your mood", he went on to say. He suggested in order to help produce more serotonin, he would prescribe some tablets. To put me at ease the doctor reiterated how common this was in young men and these tablets were to help balance my mood. It really made me feel it was quite normal and not to worry. I left the surgery with my head held a little higher than when I had walked in there. A huge weight lifted off my shoulders as now I knew help was here and I *was* going to get better. The doctor also recommended talking to someone in the form of counselling, which I began to arrange immediately. I knew I needed to talk to someone about why I was feeling down. I would do anything to feel like my old self and I knew I needed to take this advice and just do it. I normally would procrastinate and delay things by overthinking. I would have to think of how and when to do it first but I knew this was not a time to dwell. I was so proud that I had just taken the first nervous, big step towards feeling better and I had landed safely.

When I think back, it was probably the hardest thing I ever had to do. I was not used to talking about how I felt inside. Men are not taught to speak freely about how they feel. We are taught that crying is just for girls. We are taught to be strong and to be tough and not to talk about emotions. This is all so wrong. We should be able to be open and talk freely about how we feel. It is ok to feel low. It is ok to cry. It is ok to feel weak and vulnerable. We are just not used to doing it. So the thoughts of talking to someone about myself was a big thing for me, as I was an extremely private person. Just having to explain my inner feelings to anyone was a first for me. I think most of us hide so much inside it is not an easy thing to do, to show weakness as I initially saw it. I told the doctor everything as I knew deep down it would help me and my family. I wanted to be back to the person *I* liked to be around. I had lost my zest for life. I wasn't fun to be around at home. I put on a front when I was out and about but as soon as I put the key into the ignition or opened the front door I was back in the depths of despair. It was ironic that my nickname was "Smiley" and now Smiley was depressed. I hoped my life would get back on track and I felt this was the first huge step taken in order for this to happen. This was a proud day for me to get the spark back in my life and just to start to live again.

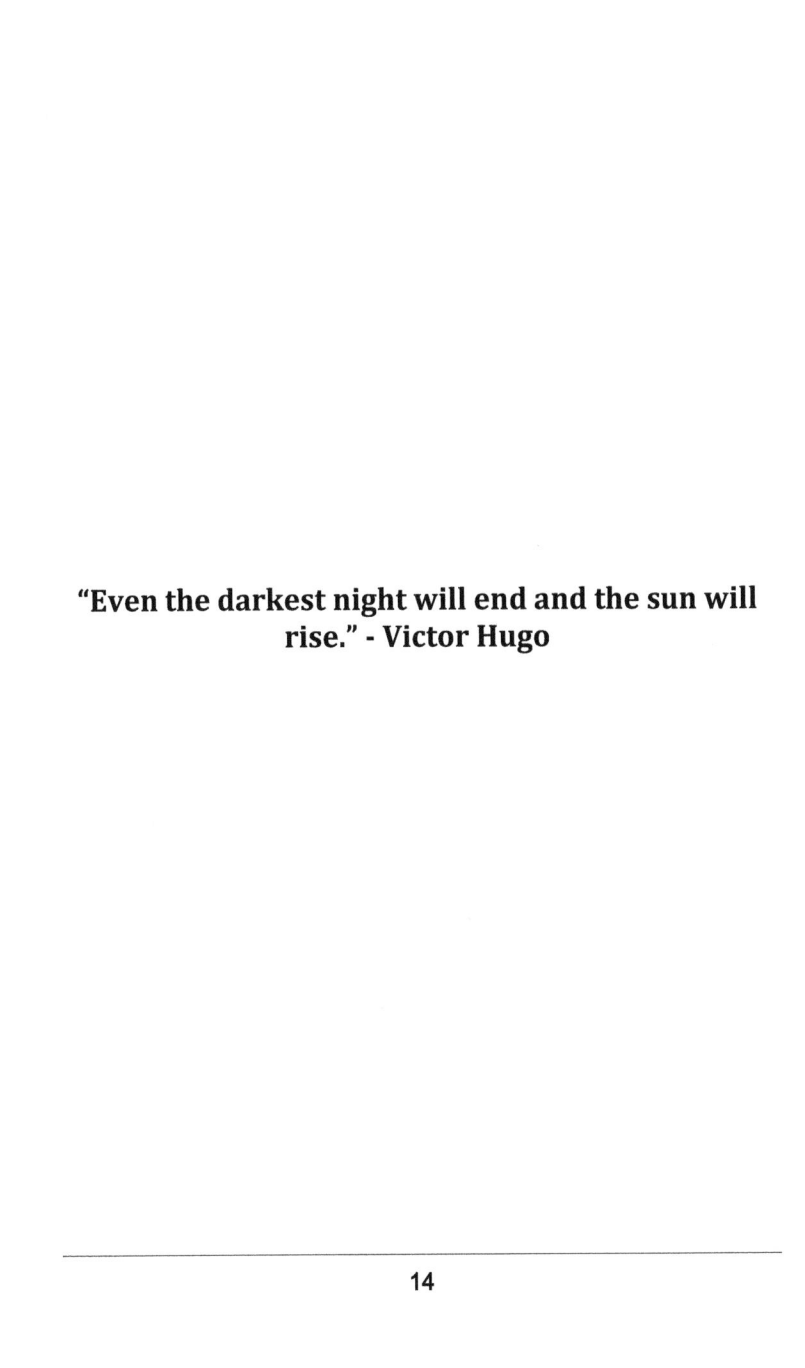

"Even the darkest night will end and the sun will rise." - Victor Hugo

Chapter 2 - Telling the Family

When I got home from the doctor's surgery, I thought it best that my parents and siblings should know why I had been so aloof of late. My first thoughts were that "ah they won't understand", so I had to think of a plan. As a typical man, we rarely discuss our feelings with anyone, unless like me it was as a last resort. Looking back, maybe that is why I ended up so depressed as I rarely spoke about feelings. I just bottled everything up from a young age. My problem was that I was always more sensitive to other people's feelings than my own and I didn't want to upset anyone. I didn't like the thoughts of anyone worrying about me. Even now, I didn't want anyone to make a song and dance about this as it was my issue to deal with. I thought of ways to let my family know but I needed to do it in my own subtle way....... then sit back and see if they would decipher it. I had just read a very honest article about a young Gaelic footballer who was very upfront about depression, so I decided I would send this article to them all via a group email. This footballer wrote a very open and frank article about how he dealt with his depression. I could really relate to everything he said and I really admired this guy for being so upfront with his emotions, how he was feeling and the thoughts he was having. So that evening when the kids were in bed, I copied the article into an email, closed my eyes and clicked the send button. I felt an instant sense of relief. I took a deep breath and felt a sense of pride again as it was a brave and positive step. Deep down I was really sending a group message where the subject field should have said 'HELP ME', but instead I wrote "Good Article". I sat there in silence for a while waiting for replies to come in. It was like fishing on a calm day and staring at the float but no movement. While I was staring at the screen I was just hoping for a bite or the penny to drop.

After a while my father replied first. I opened his reply which was a 'reply to all' and it was a very brief reply. It was his usual Galway saying, one word "Powerful". I wasn't sure if he got what I was implying but I think he just might have and he was just afraid to ask. I sat on the bed with the room in complete darkness. The bedroom was in total silence, like a lonely fisherman out for a night fish waiting to see a shimmer in the water or for another bite. As subtle as it was, I still felt that this was the easiest way to tell my family. As my eyes began to tire I said to myself 'Ok one down, four replies to go'. I thought I would log off and tomorrow is another day. It was time to go to bed. As I went to reel in my fishing rod, I suddenly got a big bite; a private message from my younger sister. She asked me straight out if I was depressed, as she had thought I might have been for awhile. I felt both shocked and a sense of relief. It was almost like getting an email that I had won something. I was excited and proud that my email did what I had intended and looked for help. I was also half stunned that my *subtle* email worked but my family knew how I operated. My cry for help got answered but I didn't know what to do next. It was like being lost on a raft at sea and finally catching the attention of a passing cargo ship. When the ship came close and threw down a ladder and then for me not to know to hide under the tarp or climb on board as I didn't know where the ship was going. I just froze. I couldn't reply to my sister as I didn't know what to say back. I didn't want to hit her with the whole truth at once as she might get a fright. I logged out and cleared my head for a while. I came to after a brief moment and whilst taking a deep breath I logged back in to see another message from the same sister apologising that she jumped the gun and didn't mean to be presumptuous. It was like the cargo ship taking back up the ladder and starting to move off after seeing nobody on the raft. I immediately replied that she was right the first time and that I was ok and dealing with it. That was a close one as I almost missed my chance.

I instantly felt better by someone else now knowing how I felt. I knew that she would support and help me, so it would give me time now to try to sort myself out and get back on the right track. Over the next few days, as families talk, I got a few messages from my other two older siblings to ask how I was, but no direct question which is the way I preferred it. I presumed news had travelled between the houses as I had hoped for. I didn't hear back from my parents but I think they now knew and they also knew how I operated . Maybe they couldn't offer any answers or didn't understand but I was just relieved they all now knew and they also knew I would be getting some support. I was happier this way as I didn't like any attention on me. I hate the spotlight. I felt it bought me time to deal with it. I wanted to tell a good friend of mine as I knew he could offer sound advice while keeping it private but for some reason I just never felt like the right time to talk. We always had a good laugh together and felt it would just bring the conversation down. It would be like going to watch a comedian on stage and then whispering to him that his dog was dead. I just enjoyed the laughs and I never wanted to dull the craic down. I do wish I told him now as I know he would have helped me. That's what friends do of course. Maybe writing this book will be my subtle way of telling my friends how low I actually was.

A few weeks passed and I began attending a counsellor after work. I went every second Tuesday for eight weeks. I used to slip in the side door and out again covertly, the way I liked it. I wasn't ashamed but just felt it was a private issue……also, being from a small town where everyone knows your business before you do. I found the counselling very tough at first. It was extremely emotional talking about how things were at home and about my family to anyone. I never really discussed my feelings before. There seemed to be a lot of frustration and even anger inside me. The years of bottling up my feelings, they just wanted to burst out but these feelings were tightly locked away so it was extremely hard to find the key. As the visits went on the tears dried up as I got things off my chest. It became easier and easier to talk without crying. It felt good to talk to someone who didn't know me. To this day I am still finding answers but I know one thing for sure, that I did feel much better every Tuesday after talking to someone who was there just to listen and not judge me. Life seemed brighter and the darkness was starting to lift.

"Bullies are always to be found where there are cowards." - Mahatma Gandhi

Chapter 3 - Back to the Beginning

Life could have been very different for me when I look back. I was born in Baldoyle, Dublin 13. I had the usual childhood playing football in the streets, popping the bubbles in the hot tar in gaps on the road on a sunny day. Getting into trouble with neighbours and chasing the bread van every week to try and take a free loaf of bread out of the open back truck. My Dad was a Garda and worked in Headquarters in Phoenix Park. He got a promotion to Sergeant which meant he was getting a transfer to a town in County Cavan. At six years old I only knew where my house and school were, never mind Cavan, but I was too young to care and saw this as an adventure. My parents sold the move to myself, my brother and my two sisters well. They said it was just like a holiday and I would see my old friends and neighbours again in a few weeks.

So that November, we all made the journey to Cavan. On the first day of school, my father brought three of us to school and off we walked in, not sure what to expect. My younger sister was only three so she would be stuck at home for another year at least. The school was much smaller than my old school in Baldoyle but everyone was very friendly. In the school corridor my brother and sister were brought to a classroom and both went in together as they were twins. I was now alone and very nervous. I was brought through the school hall and approached another classroom door. I hated being the centre of attention and dreaded what was on the other side. I was so nervous and just hoping there would be some sound lads in the class. I was brought in by the school principal. Thirty pairs of eyes stared at me. I don't think they had seen a new person join the school for quite a while. My head was firmly looking at my feet but I briefly looked up, blushed and put my head down. I was told by the class teacher to sit beside a boy who lived closest to our new house. Shane got landed with the Dub! The teacher got on with the day, lessons began and I quickly settled in. For the first few days at break times, myself and brother and sister were easy to find in the yard. We were like novelties so everytime we came out we were like new puppies and huddles formed around each of us as everyone wanted a look but to be honest everyone was very welcoming. When I think about it, back then we were probably the first Dublin family to move to the area. Everyone was so warm and friendly we felt at home in no time, just without the bread vans!

It wasn't too long before myself and my older brother joined the local scouts and, more importantly for me, the local Gaelic football team managed by the very respected and knowledgeable Parish Priest, Fr. Tom. Fr. Tom loved football and I believe back in the day when the collar was off he was a great footballer himself. We hadn't played any football in Dublin up to this. From day one, I just loved the physicality of the game. I was hooked from the first training session. I loved everything about it. It was quite a skillful game that involved some guts which I had bags of, guts that is. The skill did not come naturally as some players are born with it. I had to work hard on this part of the game. I wasn't afraid of a shoulder and loved a good tackle. I never had any fear and I would go in hard to everything and usually came out unscathed. The way that I tackled was probably more suited to rugby or maybe what you would see at a WWF wrestling match but I was working on it.... this part of my game. Gaelic was here and I loved being out on the pitch. My brother, Colin, was a year and a half older than me so we played every second year together. He played as a cornerback and I played as a corner forward. There were some decent ballers on the team. We had a few lads who could kick with both feet, the nippy left footed corner forward, a towering lad in midfield. It was a good mix and most of us hung around together and we were all friends. Being friends off the pitch was a factor in playing well. We knew each other so well that we gelled as a team. I think we all improved so much every year as we were respected and guided by Fr Tom and his passion. As we got older some of the lads shot up quickly in height. We had a few lads measuring six feet and they were only ten years old. I think they must have been eating calf nuts for breakfast. We played U8s, U10s, U12s, U14s etc so we had two years at each age group. I was very lucky as we had some very good players and we won plenty of county titles at all levels, winning leagues and championships. It was mainly the same lads so we had that understanding and team bond. We also won a few Secondary School County championships with my local school in Cavan. We really had some great teams along the way and felt lucky to be part of these great teams.

I would never say I was a great footballer but I made up for lack of skill with passion and giving everything to every game or as some people would call it "brute ignorance". Some lads could kick with both feet but my left foot was only there for emergencies but I trained hard and spent hours every evening with a ball in my hands. Soloing, hand passing and kicking the ball off the garage wall and catching it high and low. I was doing my best in school and trying to balance training, homework and a bit of study. When I got to my Leaving Cert year the workload had increased and the exams were fast approaching. With some subjects you might get away without doing homework but I was always the type of person who would not take the chance and I would stay up late to get it done. One teacher would give us two to three hours of Maths homework every night and it had to be done. If it wasn't done you could get the end of a metre stick on the knuckles and it would sting. This teacher was a great teacher so I never held a grudge as he just wanted us all to do well in the exams. We had a few teachers who would batter the head off you for any reason so I never gave them a chance or so I thought. 95% of the teachers were sound and if you played football or golf you were safe. I played both to make sure!

One teacher in particular was unpredictable and he just hated any "townies" as us local lads were called. He also only picked on small first years. So as a small first year townie I was unknowingly a target for him. I arrived in class and he locked eyes on me as he walked into the room slightly late due to my locker being at the bottom and afraid to go near the bigger students until they finished. As I sheepishly walked into the classroom, I noticed he looked irritated like he was hungover after a rough weekend. He got up quickly from his seat and he walked around at all the student desks looking for something. He was like a murderer picking his weapon of choice. He picked up a textbook but put it down when he found a much thicker textbook. He gave all the girls (who all sat on one side of the room) a wink, and walked down to the back of the classroom where myself and my fellow townies sat. We preempted what was coming as it was a Monday and we knew what he was capable of. We also had heard the stories from previous first years. We had already moved our desks back as far as they could go with our chairs resting on the radiator which left no gap for him to get in behind us. As he approached the back row he let out a roar to push our tables and chairs forward so he could get in behind us. As he walked slowly behind each one of us, he proceeded to hit the four of us with this heavy textbook. He hit us with force with the corner of the book right on the crowns of our heads. If you ducked for cover you got a punch in the ribs to make you hop up and then two or three clatters of the textbook so you had to take the hit. I was third in so he swung the book at my head and missed with his first attempt. The girls sniggered at his poor aim which made him see red. Maybe they were laughing more at me as I was trying to dodge the blows like a boxer in the ring. He went into a rage and dropped this book to the floor in anger. This weapon of choice wasn't working as he had hoped. Then in a fit of rage, he grabbed my throat with both his hands from behind. He started to tighten his grip. I thought he would let go after a few seconds but he tightened it further and stuck his fingers into my windpipe. I let out a gasp for some air. This dirty move was so unexpected that I hadn't taken a inhalation breath after dodging the textbook. I had no air in my lungs. I tried to move my head forward to get him off but I was only twelve and this was a man in his late thirties. I remember drool starting to drip uncontrollably from the side of my mouth and my eyes closing and seeing stars. My head was now as low as I could go, resting on the table. It was like I was half knocked out and also maybe half looking for mercy and for this bully to give up and stop. It was like a choke hold in a UFC fight but I wasn't going to tap out. The weight class was unfair. A heavyweight against a fly weight and the fly weight was twelve years old and taken from behind without a referee. My chair couldn't move as he was blocking me and I was pressed against the table. I thought he would give up. It was like the famous scene in the movie 'The Revenant' when the bear was attacking Leonardo DiCaprio. The rest of the class sat in silence and in pure shock with this first attack. Like in the movie when you thought the bear had enough damage done and him lying there in bits, the next ferocious attack happened. His hands still gripped around my neck, he shook my neck up and down, hitting my forehead off the desk three or four times before letting go. I gasped for air, it was like finding a hole in the ice after being trapped underwater. I was weak and blurry and so confused as to why I was attacked by a teacher for no reason but only to try to impress his audience. He walked up the classroom smiling at the girls and went back over and sat on their desks chatting about the weekend. He eventually began his class like nothing had happened. I was told by everyone who had encountered him not to bother reporting him as the Principal would do nothing and the bully teacher will make your life hell for the rest of the year. I went home disheartened and angry that this person who should have been there to teach, was really only there to bully little children to feel better about himself. I was afraid to tell my parents as I knew they would say that I must have been doing something to deserve it. I stayed quiet and bottled up that anger.

I came back to school the following September. I was in second year and now bigger and stronger after a summer of growth. I was actually hoping this "teacher" would try what he did again but he stayed well away. I learned that, as I said earlier, he only bullied and hit small first year students. What a coward I thought. Over the years we heard of all the first years he hit and he almost broke one boy's arm when he was supervising an Engineering class. He thought one boy was being cheeky so he grabbed him and put his arm in a metal vice and tightening this boy's arm until he almost broke it. Unfortunately this bully was never fired and was teaching in the same school for years where he continued to terrorize all the first years students. For years I had hoped to meet this teacher in a dark alley as I am sure dozens of first years felt the same. To think a person who was there to try to teach us, only gained pleasure by physically hurting us. He made me start to distrust people more but maybe he taught me a valuable lesson that would help me later in life - let Karma deal with him. I actually hope he reads this to show what an absolute bully he was and that will be my sense of justice.

"All our dreams can come true, if we have the courage to pursue them." - Walt Disney

Chapter 4 - County Call Up

One quiet evening the house phone rang and it was a call for me. It was the Cavan County Minor football manager asking me to come into the County Minor squad. It was one of those moments you dreamed of. I was thrilled. A few weeks later, training began and a bus was sent to collect all the players from all over my side of the county. I was given a day and time and asked to be out at the end of the road and the bus would be going by at a certain time. I knew lads from other local clubs and once I saw them all I knew I was with a squad of decent footballers. As always, I had my doubts if I could compete alongside these lads but I would give it everything to make the final squad. A few challenge games were planned as the squad needed to be cut down. Players would be cut from the panel as the weeks went on. Match day one arrived and I would get to don the royal blue jersey. The manager called out the team and I held my breath "Wing half forward, Niall McHugo". The elation inside was just surreal. I didn't show it and I kept my poker face on as if I was expecting it. I was handed the number ten jersey and I put it on with such pride.

Looking back now, this was one of the proudest moments for me. It really was a dream come true to put on my county jersey and to be told by the manager before the game "you are the best player in your position in the county at this level". The hairs on my neck stood up and it felt so good even though I wasn't sure if it was 100% true, but it was a serious pep talk nonetheless. I always doubted myself and my ability and even when I was told this, I played it down and I didn't let myself believe it. To play for your county team is the dream for any young footballer growing up and I was so proud. This first game was an away game against Longford. I played ok and scored a decent point off a break at midfield. I took a few solos on my right foot and from about thirty five yards out I kicked the ball and it just crept over the bar with inches to spare. I was relieved and nice to get a score on my debut. The manager seemed happy enough but he was a very hard man to read. The next game came and I think again I held my own. It was against neighbours and rivals, Meath. I scored another point and I worked hard off the ball making runs and just got stuck in. This game was just across the Cavan border, which was ideal as it wasn't too far away from home. The pitch was only ten minutes away from my house, so it wouldn't take up half the day like other away games did. I did all I could on the pitch so I just hoped I did enough to stay in the squad for the league and championship which wasn't too far away.

I didn't come from a traditional footballing family. My Dad was from South County Galway and he played a bit of hurling. His claim to fame is playing hurling in New York but funny enough he played for Kilkenny when they played a game against Galway - he might not want anyone to know this! But Gaelic football was my passion. My family rarely came to watch me play but I never really let it get to me. I couldn't blame them because standing in the cold, early on a Sunday morning when sometimes the games would be low scoring, was probably not the most exciting thing to do. . Deep down I would really have liked to have seen them there to support me and to cheer me on, even the odd game. I never complained as I knew they were all busy and they had their own interests.

One evening I got a phone call and it was word that I had made the final Cavan squad for the league. Unfortunately, the Leaving Cert was also fast approaching and the homework was increasing by the week so I had to make a seriously tough decision. I doubted if I could do both. I needed someone to encourage me that I could manage both, as I always doubted myself. I told my parents that I had made the squad but it wasn't the reaction I had hoped for. My father thought it best that I put my studies first as he saw that football was taking up too much of my spare time. My head dropped as I really wanted to be able to do both. To this day I still remember the phone call I had with the manager. He phoned me one day to tell me his plans for the league and championship and where I would be playing. I would be starting as he saw me as an important player in the team. I waited for a gap in the conversation and I broke the news to him that I had to drop out. I can still hear his voice getting louder when I told him that I couldn't join the squad. He asked me to reconsider but my mind had been made up whether it was the right call or not and I hung up the phone. Looking back I don't know if I or my father was right to make that call but my father wanted me to do well in my studies and get into University. I still regret that decision to this day as how many times do you get a chance to play for your County? Not every footballer gets to live this dream. I just wish I could have balanced both my studies and football and maybe convinced my Dad I could do it. Maybe I didn't even put up a fight and I didn't tell him how much it meant to me due to me always doubting my own ability. Then who's to say I might not have got the University course I wanted if I continued to play on. Lots of unknowns, and yes I could have been dropped later in the year if I played a poor game or two.

To make myself feel better about this decision, I thought of being stuck on a bench up in North Donegal on a wet Sunday evening with a three hour bus drive home ahead of me. Yes I am making it sound as bad as I can, so I can feel better about my decision. Ah well......but I always wondered if that was to be my only chance to play with the county and I threw it away. I never really told anyone that I played a few games for Cavan, as I just didn't like the attention but also felt like I didn't deserve the kudos. I suppose most people wouldn't believe me if I said I played as a wing forward for Cavan, especially if they saw my accuracy in front of the goalposts as the years went on.

The Leaving Cert came and it all went well enough to get accepted into the course I wanted. Maybe my father was right afterall. I got a place at The University of Limerick and I was looking forward to four years of what college life had to offer and the adventures that lay ahead.

"Talent wins games, but teamwork and intelligence wins championships."
- Michael Jordan

Chapter 5 – Winning Championships was Easy

Before starting in college I began my first year playing with our second senior team or the reserves as they were called. They were more commonly known as The Junior B Team or some of us called them 'The Killer B's'! It was a bit of an eclectic mix of players. In describing the team, it probably would be easier to picture a movie about a football team formed in a prison. You have a few lads of all shapes and sizes aged from 17 to 47. Our goalkeeper used to have a fag for his warm up and then kept them close by when things got quiet during the game. He would hand his packet of fags to the umpire to mind and he could smoke away once the ball was kicked out up the other end of the field. We had some fairly overweight lads scattered around the team but they were more agile and skilful than they looked. We had some big lads on the forward line so all we had to do was get the ball into them. They would do the rest and generally without looking, they would stick the ball into the top corner of the net. They had an unbelievable eye for goal and they just knew where it was. The one rule they had was…… just don't make them run! The ball had to be kicked into their chests. Then a little dummy and bang! GOAL! Mixed in with these experienced lads, were some of us young quick and fit lads. We had a nice little team and a great mix of talent, fitness and experience. What really made the team stronger, was that we had great craic at training. We had big numbers arriving for training every night which meant we could have a full size game every night, fifteen on fifteen. This was so important as the managers could try different game plays and positions plus it also put pressure on everyone to keep their places on the team. For any team, competition for places is so important, as it keeps everyone on their toes. If you missed a training session or had a poor game, someone could step in and take your place.

We had some great managers who always encouraged and got the very best out of every player. I remember this one manager who treated us like his own children. He brought us to games in the back of his jeep no matter how many of us there were. We would all squeeze in and we sat on hay bales in the back. He could have more than half the team in the jeep and the craic was mighty. After the games he would always buy us poor students a few drinks. He filled us with praise and built up our confidence to no end. He just loved the club and we respected him so much as he went out of his way to make sure we played and were all enjoying football. In that first year with the Killer B's, we went on to win the Junior B championship. We followed that up with another one the following year. Two championships in my first two years with my club was an unbelievable start. These championships *seemed* easy enough to come by. I could get used to this winning feeling and the elation, not to mention the partying afterwards. The feeling you get when the final whistle blows of a final is just so hard to explain, pure elation. My heart would burst through my chest and I would be totally speechless. Euphoric is probably the only way I can describe it! To win a championship for my home town at such a young age was surreal. I was only starting my football career while other older club legends were finishing theirs. It was an honour to play with these lads who had won one or more senior championships. Some of these lads had many miles in the legs but they loved the game and they still togged out to help bring us young lads on. They gave it their all in the games and the mix of us young lads doing the running and these lads having the experience and the cuteness.....it was a perfect mix and it worked. Most importantly they looked after us when you had a big brute of lad edging close to give ya a clip off the ball. These lads would save the day and stand in the middle and take over. It was like having a personal bodyguard or two on the pitch. Anyone who tried to have a go at any young lad would know all about it in a few seconds. We could stand back, exhale and let them at it. Protecting the young lads was like an unwritten rule that our club had and I still see it on the pitch today.

Back then when I was seventeen years old, the pinnacle of any footballer's medal hoard was the dream of a senior championship medal with your local club. This was a dream of mine since I saw my team winning the senior championship in 1992. They were heroes to us lads playing under-age football at the time. I dreamt of standing in the centre of my home town with the crowd roaring as the Anglo Celt Cup was passed about. Someday for sure I thought......and hoped to see that day! If junior championships were this easy, surely I could win a senior championship?

For the next year or so I played Junior League and championship with passion and pride and I always gave it 100%. I remember one of my first Junior B games against a tough club. A big midfielder caught the ball out in space, so I made a bee line for him and hit him a shoulder as hard as I could. I think he just about noticed me hitting him. It was probably a bit like a fly crashing into a cow, but the crowd seemed to like my enthusiasm and let out a cheer as they could see I had some fire in me. It felt like the Gladiators in the Colosseum and we were there to entertain the crowd. When the crowd cheered, I liked this reaction so I did my best to ensure they were cheering more and more. I was willing to entertain them if I could, after all they had paid in to see us defeat the other side, just without the swords, spears and lions. Later in the same game I got my first awakening of what Junior B football could be like. I collected a pass and turned for goal. I could feel the breath of the full back behind me and the grunt and profanities as he tried to catch me. He knew I was faster than him as I was probably one third his weight. As I bore down on goal and just the keeper to beat, I went to pull the trigger, but this brute (from behind) stuck his studs into my ankle bone and down I went in a heap. I heard the whistle sound so I knew I got a penalty. I dusted myself off and examined the damage. I could see blood had come through my sock, so I knew it wasn't great. My ankle had two deep cuts from his metal studs and it swelled up immediately. I pulled back up my sock and hobbled off to watch the penalty to be taken. It was converted so it felt better knowing I got justice for the horror tackle and we would go three points clearer on the scoreboard. I knew my ankle was bad but I decided to jog it off. I didn't want to show this guy I was hurt as I knew he would have loved it if I had to go off, as he needed a rest. These injuries don't hurt until you cool down, so the damage was only really more evident as the evening went on. I couldn't walk on my ankle that night but I knew a week's rest and a bit of ice and I would be back in action again soon. I was already annoyed I would miss training or the next game which meant my position could be taken.

On normal match days, the second football team (The Killer B's) played before the first team. The senior manager would be there to watch the reserves to see who was playing well. After the first game was over you walked into the dressing room which was full of the first team, ready to go out onto the pitch for the main event. When you played well in the first game for the reserves, you would get a tap on the shoulder and told "leave the boots on" and you would be thrown a sub jersey for the senior team. This was such an honour! You gave a nod back, swapped your old muddy, sweat laden jersey for a fresh dry one, took a swig out of a drink and out ya went again for round two. As you jogged onto the pitch, the crowds would be starting to come in then with the main match close to throw in. As the pitch was tight the supporters were nearly on the sidelines. I could always hear some of the supporters whispering and asking who the young lads were like "Is that young McHugo?" Some would even be shouting your name with some encouragement like a superstar! It felt good to think they wanted me to do well for the team. That first day I was given a jersey, I went on to make my senior football team debut. It was against a strong hard hitting team. I was brought on and sent in as a wing forward with about ten or fifteen minutes left. It was a tight game with just a point or two in it so it could have gone either way. When I ran on, I couldn't believe the pace and intensity of the game. It was frantic and I had absolutely no time to think. I won a break from midfield and three of the opposition were on me like flies on shite, battering me from all angles. I held on tight, took the blows and won the free. I was now baptised into senior football and I loved it. We held out for the win which was a great feeling and I hoped I did enough to keep my name on the mind of the manager for the following weekend.

That September, I began University in Limerick so I began to travel up from Limerick at weekends to play games. It didn't really bother me as it was all part of being on a football team. A college mate of mine played for Donegal hurlers and his journey was twice the distance of mine and he didn't miss a weekend so my journey wasn't as bad compared to him. Over the years one manager tried me as a defender, so I now found myself in the backs after so many years as a forward. I was young and fit so I didn't mind where I played. I usually played wing back, as I had the fitness to get up and down the wings. Then as the years went on, I was rooted in at full back. This was a big deal to me. Firstly it is a central position but also the last line of defence. It was particularly special to me, as my club hero played there and I now had his boots to fill which I would try to do as best I could. I had a legend in goals behind me guiding me all the way. There were not many better men to have guide you and keep you on your toes. He would be constantly giving instructions to me. "Smiley left....Smiley right"..... and of course the praise and encouragement if and when needed. He was the best in the business and I had a lot of time for him as he was so passionate and just like me he loved to win. He was a gentle giant and as strong as an ox. In training and pre-match warm ups he would often block shots with his forearm and then send the ball back about twenty five yards. I remember in one game in Breffni Park, he was stopping shots when another one of the lads drove the ball towards goal. He was focusing on another ball and this ball hit him at full force in the side of the head. The lad who took the shot had the hardest shot of the team and was under twenty yards out from goal when he took his shot. Our keeper stumbled but never hit the ground. He looked dazed and he was definitely concussed. His eyes were rolling around but he played the whole game. At half time he didn't remember playing the first half and he even asked what the score was. There were no head injury assessments (HIAs) back then or anyone to make that call.

I tried to balance football with college life which was hard as I could never stay in Limerick on weekends. I was always on the lunchtime bus on a Friday to make Friday evening training. It is not a hassle when you love something. I looked forward to the weekends and putting on the black and amber of my club and the number three jersey. I always did my best and hoped to have a decent game with the aim of keeping my man scoreless or with as few scores as I could. It was very easy knowing how you played when you got back to the dressing rooms after the final whistle. The way to tell if you played well was when the retired legends of the club walked into the dressing room straight after the games and they gave you the slap on the top of the head. My head was always looking down as I tried to catch my breath after a tough battle. While it was there I would examine the war wounds and scrape the blood and mud from my legs. After each slap I would look up but almost knew who it was by the voice. I would give them a modest nod, smile and a thumbs up. When these lads said "well done" or "mighty game", it was like an adrenaline rush and the cuts and bruises didn't feel as sore after that. The harder the slap on the head the better you played. It was a tradition and it was the only time that I welcomed a hard slap. I respected these legends who won medals for our club and they were as passionate now as they were when they themselves donned the jersey.

"A journey of a thousand miles begins with a single step." – Lao Tzu

Chapter 6 - Coming to America

During my four college years, part of the course involved two work placements with companies linked to the University. These would be for half the academic year in year two and year four. The first of these opportunities came around so I had to think where I wanted to work. We would have a choice of companies based all around Ireland or America. I was nineteen and the chance to go to America was too big to turn down. I told myself I would apply for some American jobs and if I got an offer I would make a decision then. Most of my class applied for jobs around Limerick or Dublin. Some had girlfriends at home so that ruled America out for them. I was single and I had no ties. The interviews came and I got an offer for a job in Boulder, Colorado. Yes Mork and Mindy country! I thought about it and I couldn't turn it down so I accepted it and I was off that February. Nobody else in my class was going to Colorado. Some got jobs in Boston and New York so I was off with five other third year business students. I wouldn't be long getting to know them.

We arrived safe and sound and we were collected in a limo and brought to our apartments. We had two apartments in a student block with three of us in each. I shared with a guy from Limerick and one other girl. Three other girls took the other apartment. Over the next few weeks we were trained up in selling rail tickets in a call centre to Americans . We had to learn the system and train timetables and how to book an overnight train. We had the weekends off so we made sure to party hard and as it was ski season we made sure to get up the Rocky Mountains for a ski before the season ended. I arrived up a slope, no lessons taken and off I went. I saw a few people stop so I knew I could do that. I remember bombing down at what felt like a hundred miles and hour and just towards the end of the run, I would make a sharp turn and spray snow on anyone below and come to a complete stop. I probably looked like a pro but I had no idea. It was such an adrenaline rush going so fast and zig zagging down the powdery slopes.

We settled in very quickly as everyone we worked with really made us feel at home. We were even given a free car by an elderly couple who had one to spare. Having a car allowed us to explore more. When we finished up on a Friday we would pack up and get on the road. One weekend we drove to the Grand Caynon. We flew into San Fransisco for another weekend... and a drive into Denver wasn't too far to watch The Rockies play some baseball. Life was good and my fake ID meant I could drink with the others as I was the youngest of the six being a year behind them. All was going great until I lost my ID in the back of a taxi. Shazbot! Now we had a problem. My brother posted me his old ID and I changed the picture. It didn't look great but it was worth a try. Some niteclubs allowed Under 21's in but they couldn't access the bar but the others would feed straws through the mesh so I could drink away. One night in Denver I got stopped for ID. I showed them my fake ID with my brother Colin's name on it. The bouncer asked me to verify this with a bank card. I showed them my bank card with 'Niall

McHugo' on it. He looked suspiciously at it and said "Hold on.....Which one are you? Colin or Niall?" I thought on my feet and explained that Niall was Irish for Colin and I held my breath. He looked up and broke into a smile and said "Right on" and gave my a high five and in I went!

As we settled in we said we would check out some Irish bars in Denver where we met some expats. They asked if we would like to come and play some GAA with the local club, Denver Gaels. Now that we had a car we said we would and started training. We met so many people so quickly. If the girls had the car we would always have a lift. I remember getting a lift with an English guy in this almighty banger of a car - it was literally falling apart. One day on the way back from Denver the heavens opened but the car was missing something. The wipers didn't work! We were travelling down a five or six lane motorway or "freeway"... but we had already improvised. We had tied a shoelace to the driver side wiper and in sync myself and the driver pulled the lace over and back until the rain stopped. We made it home safe and sound.

The girls trained for an hour and then us men trained. We really enjoyed it and were made to feel very welcome straight away. The older players really looked after us and made sure we all had jobs. The work was going well and we joined the company softball team. Anything that involves drinking beer while playing sport has to be fun. The Americans loved us and we all hit our sales targets every week.

Every American person we met was half or quarter Irish. One lady told me she was half Irish and I always asked what part of Ireland. Her reply will never be forgotten. She said her family was from The Isle of Man. I smiled but didn't want to ruin her joy of being one eighth Irish. St Patricks Day was our day and I never celebrated as much. Funny how you are more Irish once you leave Ireland! I spent most of my day telling Americans it's Saint Patrick's Day or St. Paddy's Day and NOT Saint Patty's Day. They didn't care and continued to call it Patty!

As the season went on, the club were asking if we would be still around in August as the US GAA Finals were on in Washington. Myself and Kieran (the Limerick lad) agreed we would stay to play. As ours was the only club in Denver we automatically qualified. That August we flew to Washington and did a few tourist things. We met up with the team for a pint or two but we had an early night with the first game the next day. It was a knockout competition so we wanted to try to do as well as we could. We were drawn against Washington so we knew they would have a huge crowd cheering them on. The pitch was rock hard, like concrete and my knees were already in bits from playing softball with my employer company. I used to slide to steal bases so it took its toll on my knees. As we lined out we were missing our captain. He was 6ft 4" and a superb footballer. Word had it that he had a late night on the beer and had not surfaced from his bed. Just as the game was about to start Lazarus appeared but he looked shook. He took his place in midfield and within ten or fifteen minutes he punched his marker and was shown red. Our game was over as he ran the show. We kept the game close and lost by just a few points. Our US GAA championships was over but amazing to say that I played in one.

My time was up in America after this and we made a quick trip to New York before catching our flight back to Shannon. "Nanu Nanu" to America! On the flight I was starting to think of getting back to college and back to football again. I was glad I kept my fitness up while I was in America so I knew I could get back into it in no time.

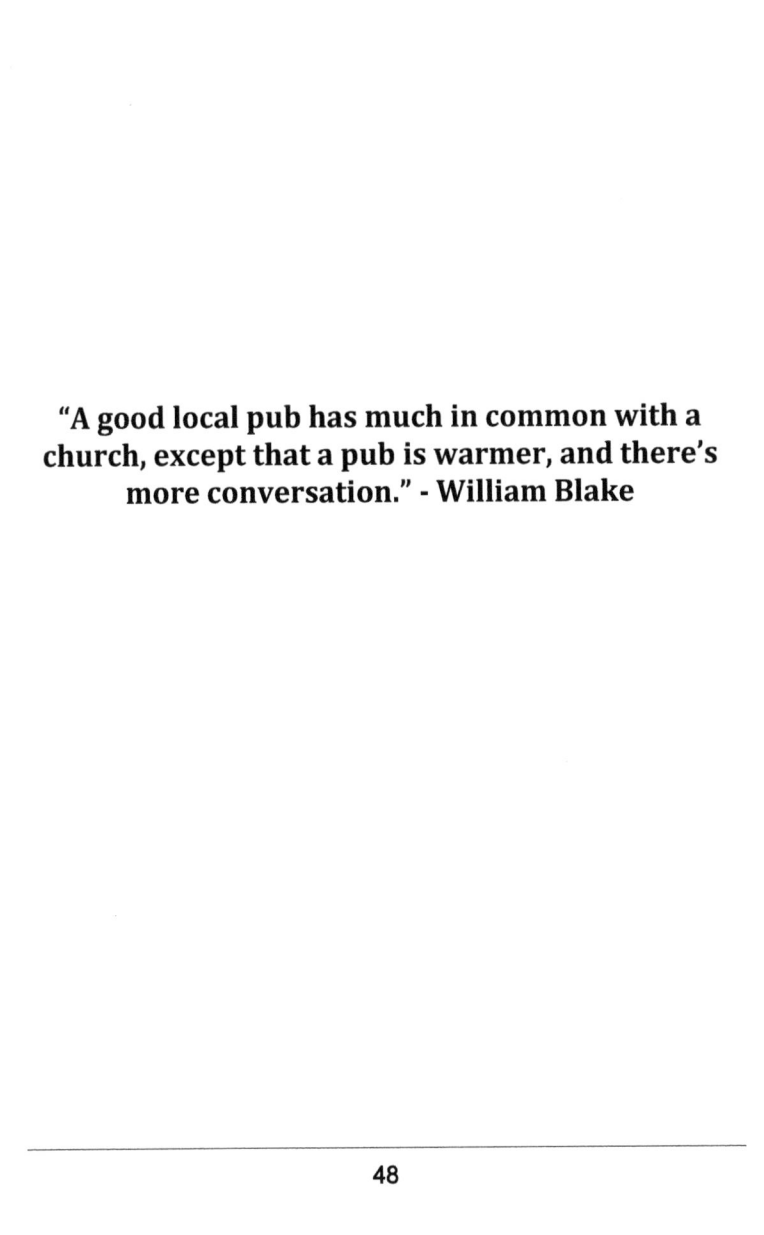

"A good local pub has much in common with a church, except that a pub is warmer, and there's more conversation." - William Blake

Chapter 7 - Social Side of Football - The Pub

After each weekend game, the tradition was to have 'a pint or two' in the local pub whether it was home or away. If it was an away game you knew you wouldn't be staying for the night but we always had a few pints to quench the thirst. You would be side by side drinking a pint with a lad who only a half hour ago you were in battle with and about to kill each other. In the pub and on the pitch we were both foaming at the mouth for different reasons (depending on the service). I suppose when forty players and maybe sixty of the supporters all walk into a pub at 2pm on a Sunday and all want drinks at the same time, it takes a while to serve everyone! The supporters usually had their drinks and were in the middle of ordering their second by the time we got showered and in to join them. When the players got to the pub, no fights ever carried from the pitch to the pub. In fact it was quite the opposite. If you spotted a guy you got a clip or gave a clip to, a handshake of respect was more the norm and all was forgiven. It was a lovely tradition which not only supported the local pubs but was a place to discuss the match with everyone.

This tradition is nearly gone now, with the stricter drink driving laws and in fairness you can't argue with that. If only you could get a few non drinking players, but they were like hens teeth back then anyway! Lucky for me I didn't have a car back then so I always had a driver to bring me back home. After leaving the pub on away match days, we may have to pass through another town. You might spot your teammates or some supporters' cars parked outside a pub and an unplanned pit stop was made for a quick one before getting back home. If you did stop you might meet the local team in there drinking after their own game so the banter and slagging was mighty. Absolute great comradery between all clubs and it is something you would find only in GAA. There was no Twitter back then so that was the way results from the other games were shared and liked.

Eventually we would make it back to our own local pub where the drinks continued, win, lose or draw. We would re-examine the game over and over, especially when we lost. I had moved to Dublin by now so I had less of a journey back. On many a Sunday with work looming the next day, I would get whoever was driving from the game to pull up at my home place. I would quickly pop in, say my goodbyes, grab my clothes for the week and jump back into the car only to make it as far as my local pub. The bags would be thrown in the corner and pints ordered. I remember the odd Sunday, my Dad would pop in for a quiet evening pint and I would have to tell him I was getting the late bus! The look he gave me showed he knew what I was really at and he never caused a fuss as he could see the craic was good! The bus to Dublin would usually have to wait until early Monday when I surfaced after crashing on a friend's couch. Productivity at work on a Monday was never the best of the week.

After obtaining my university degree I started to work in Dublin over the next seven years. I drove home every Tuesday and Friday night for training. There was no motorway back then so it took up to two hours on the old N3. I dreaded the traffic coming into Dunshaughlin as it backed up at rush hour. I didn't think anything of the trip as it was all part of the deal if you wanted to play. Everyone had sacrifices to give. I have to say it *was* a struggle some nights, but this is what I wanted to do. Some people questioned why I would drive up and down twice a week, miss weekends away, miss parties and skip after work drinks. I knew these people wouldn't understand as they never played GAA and they didn't realise this is what needs to be done by the full squad if you want to play football and try competing in leagues and championships. I was playing good football and my old junior manager even told me that the county senior team was monitoring me about a possible call up to the Cavan senior team. This was my boyhood dream but I wasn't sure if it was ever true or maybe he was just continuing to build my confidence like he did as my manager years before. Years went by and I was getting fed up with the rat race in Dublin. Dublin was a cold place compared to home. Every Sunday evening, tired and bruised after a game, then getting packed up and driving through town and watching all my friends having a pint outside the local. All the while I was going back to a dodgy cold flat in Drumcondra. I really wanted to have their social life and home life. It was time to think and devise a plan to get home.

I needed a change of job. I was being bullied by a manager at my job at the time. She was so horrible to me. She was going through a divorce and I think she brought her anger to work with her and projected it on to me, the only male on the team. I was the youngest member of staff and she knew I was an easy target. I was so young and naive I didn't know what to do and just soaked up her daily negative comments. I worked so hard, never missed a day but she could only criticise while she sat doing nothing all day. As you can imagine the morale in the job was starting to drop, so it could be the time to bail. Maybe I needed a break or something new. I never thought of travelling but over the next few months I heard that two of my teammates were planning on travelling to Australia. It got me thinking. This could be a way out of Dublin and maybe a way to get back home eventually. I sent the official letter to HR to request a career break for the end of the year when the football season would be finished. I waited for a few weeks for my reply but luckily enough my career break was granted. I was told I could take a maximum of twelve months off work which was perfect. I was thrilled as I really felt this was the start of a new chapter for me. It didn't take long to book my tickets. On December 28th I was off on my travels to Oz via Asia.

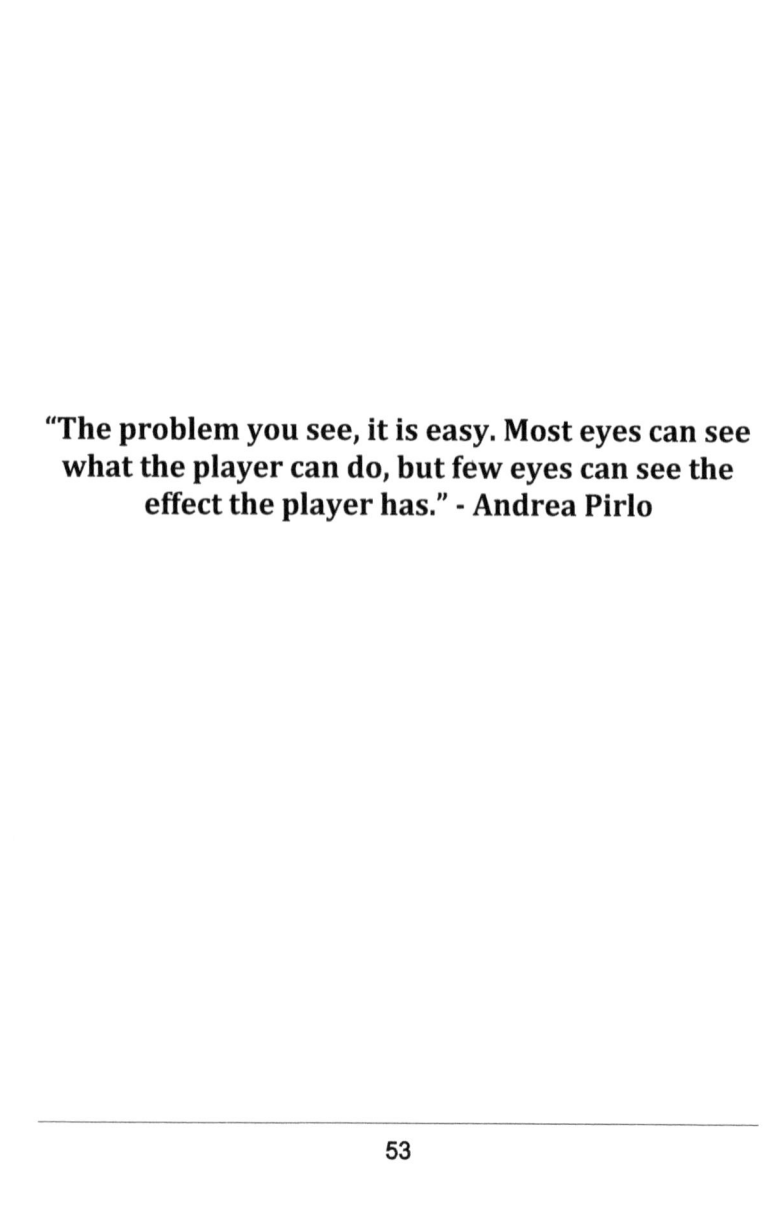

"The problem you see, it is easy. Most eyes can see what the player can do, but few eyes can see the effect the player has." - Andrea Pirlo

Chapter 8 - Oz and Back

When I was about 28 years old half the country was either coming or going to Australia. Some people loved it and they never came home and some hated it, so there was only one way to find out. I needed to get this 'travel thing' out of my system. Myself and the lads planned our flights and we aimed to spend six to eight weeks travelling around Asia before flying into Perth. Our first flight was Dublin to Bangkok. I was with friends in Bangkok which is a very busy spot, full of tourists. We hit a few bars down Koh San Road and settled ourselves whilst trying to learn some of the essential Thai language. We just needed a few useful words like "Hello", "Thank you", "Beer Please" and "Goodbye". The rest could be done by pointing plus the locals knew enough English with all the tourists there. We did our fair share of drinking but we had made plans to see the country too. We did a two day hike up a mountain and stayed in a village on the summit. The view and especially the sunset was just breathtaking. We visited local temples and famous landmarks.

One day we saw a sign for white water rafting so we said we would give it a go. We were collected by bus and we were brought to a local river and kitted out with a life jacket and brought to our inflatable raft. I had rafted a few times over the years and after only a few minutes I realised that I had more experience than the guide. His job was to control the direction of the dinghy, keep us safe and away from rocks but I don't think he knew what he was at. As we travelled along the river we hit every rock and boulder on the river. It was like he was aiming for them. We even lodged behind a few rocks and needed help to get out. It was a disaster! At one stage he directed us straight into a rock at speed and we hit it with such force we all flew head over heels into the water. One of the lads couldn't swim so he went into a panic splashing away thinking he was about to drown. I saw him splashing so I quickly swam over to him and grabbed him by the front of the lifejacket and held him up. I told him he was ok and swam him back over to the raft and pushed him back in. At this stage the other lads had managed to crawl back into the dinghy. As I went to get on board a powerful current took my legs and pulled me with force away from the raft. It was like it was in slow motion when you know this isn't going to end well. The current was too strong and down the rapids I went. I went under, hit rocks and emerged for a breath before being pulled under again swallowing mouthfuls of dirty, yellow river water. I resurfaced now and again and tried to see what was ahead. I saw a massive rock coming towards me so my plan was to try to cling on to it with my arms and legs but it was covered in algae. I couldn't get a grip and my hands slipped and off down the river I went again. I was thinking the worst and annoyed with myself for being too complacent in the water. I honestly thought this was the way I was going to die and I was so angry with myself for treating this dangerous river with no respect. I thought about my family and how my father always warned us as children about the sea, currents and to be careful, and I didn't heed his advice. I thought about how I should have got into the raft quicker once I knew my friend was safe but that extra second I took to grab the rope had now caused me to be in serious danger. As I got weaker and didn't know how much longer I had, the water suddenly calmed. I didn't delay this time and I swam as hard as I could towards the shore. I made it but I was wiped. I sat on the stones and got my breath back and I felt so relieved and blessed. A few minutes later, the raft arrived with a very relieved and panic stricken guide. He probably took so long to get to me as I am sure he hit a few more rocks on the way down. My friends didn't even look as worried as he was. I got back on board and after a bit of slagging we finished the last part of the river which was a very quiet affair for me. I checked my body and my legs were cut up but all limbs intact so I knew I would be fine. I learned a valuable lesson that day, don't mess with water. There is a fine line between bravery and stupidity. Bravery on the pitch was always one of my strengths and I was glad it kicked into action to help my team mate but almost at my own cost. It reminded me of how much sacrifice players make for their teams, where they put their head on the line, get injured, push themselves so much it hurts but it doesn't seem like it is a negative thing. I know if you asked players, they wouldn't change a thing despite the bent fingers, arthritis, back pain, new hips and dodgy knees.

After that incident I recalled the last time I was in Thailand. I was in a small two propeller aircraft travelling to one of the Thai islands. We were all hungover and everyone was asleep apart from myself. I was looking out the window at the views when I noticed one of the propellers started to slow down. I thought I was imagining things as there was no commotion at all but then everyone was asleep. I waited and waited for something to happen and then the propeller just stopped. Immediate panic hit me but there was nobody around to ask or see if I was dreaming. Eventually the captain came on and told everyone in a very calm voice that the aircraft was down to one working engine so the flight would take an hour longer. My heart was in my mouth for the rest of the flight. I stared at the working engine for the remainder of the flight until we landed and then I could breathe again. When we landed we were escorted by a dozen emergency vehicles with red flashing lights. I think the plane may have been in more danger than we were told but we landed and never asked any more questions. Maybe I need to stop visiting Thailand!

A few days after this adventure, we travelled using buses and planes to see as much of Vietnam, Laos and Cambodia as we could. I loved history, especially the Vietnam War, so now to be able to crawl in the Cú Chi Tunnels in the forests in Vietnam made by the VietCong was an unbelievable feeling. To be walking where over 58,000 American soldiers were sent to their deaths was an eerie feeling. Two of my favourite movies were 'Platoon' and 'Full Metal Jacket' so it made being there more surreal. When you walk around the jungles in Vietnam you will find old American tanks scattered along the forest where they were blown up or immobilised in some way. There are also many shooting ranges run by the military where you can shoot from any type of gun or machine gun. You can feel like Rambo for a few minutes shooting an M60 machine gun at a target. When you finish shooting you could get called over by another guy in uniform. It was all done very covertly and it reminded me of getting offered illegal fireworks on Henry Street in October. This guy looks around suspiciously and asks you if you would like to throw a grenade and try to blow up a duck in a small lake. This was obviously not something they could advertise or it was a little side hustle to make more money from tourists. He then asks if you would like to shoot a rocket launcher. I was content after shooting from heavy machine guns and I also didn't fancy blowing up a defenceless duck with a grenade! I took off my red bandanna and washed the black stripes off my face and that was as close it got to being a soldier for me. It must have been an unbelievable feeling shooting those heavy guns in a battle with bullets whizzing past you from all angles. The feeling of not knowing if you would be killed or ambushed everyday you set off! I already had my near death experience and that was enough for anyone. Huge respect to any soldier who fought in wars and who got out alive.

In the next few days we continued our trip and travelled on to Cambodia. Here we went to Angkor Wat which is a twelfth century temple and an architect's dream. A few days later we were standing sombrely in the Killing Fields in Cambodia. This is where a brutal genocide in the mid 1970's saw nearly two million people killed by Pol Pot and the Khmer Rouge. Anyone deemed an intellect was killed in the worst mass killing of the twentieth century. Eight thousand human skulls of innocent people are stacked in a glass shrine and it stuns you into silence.

On our last leg we finished up in Laos which has some party spots to stop off in. The best thing to do is 'River Tubing' where you are given an inflated tractor tube and driven in an open back truck to a river and off you go down the river. You float down the river and stop off at bars along the route back to town. At these bars there would be beach volleyball and high zip lines where you could jump into the water. The crowd would watch and cheer for good landings or crazy flips from the zip line. My landings were awful and I could hear the crowd groan as I smashed the water on my side. As the partying continued along our river journey, time got away from us and we still had a big distance to get to the bottom of the river and the sun was setting quickly. Alcohol and playing in water is never a good mix but we made it to the bottom in total darkness. Local taxi drivers would wait for any late tubers to float by and they would bring you back to your accommodation.

We got back into Bangkok with a day or two to spare before our flights to Australia. When we returned that evening to Bangkok the Thai Army was all over the city. Bangkok was on high alert due to bomb threats from a militant group, so tensions were high. Army officers with machine guns were on every road and all main tourist roads were closed to traffic. There was a real sense of unease around the city. We didn't really know what was going on or if it was a regular occurrence, so I felt uncomfortable. That night there were a few explosions but not near where we were, so we got out unscathed.

The next day we took our flights to Perth for the second and main part of our travels. I visited a few old school friends who lived near Perth before buying my car and hitting the road to start seeing the real Australia. I said my goodbyes to the lads from home but I would be meeting them again at a few stages during the year. I travelled around and everything was going great. Western Australia is so unspoilt and very barren. You always needed a full tank of petrol before leaving a town as you could use a full tank before you reach the next petrol station. The scenery was amazing with wild emus, camels, kangaroos roaming around not to mention the huge Huntsman spiders. One of the highlights for me was when I took a 4 day self guided canoe trip from a town in Northern Australia called Kununurra. No tour guide with us. Just a group of tourists and a map with the route and camping spots marked where to stop each evening. All the equipment was provided so we just needed to bring food and drinks. It was a 55 km paddle down the Ord River. I remember before we set off, the owner of the hostel pointed to a poster on the notice board. It was a warning about the sighting of a saltwater crocodile so he told us all not to swim along a certain section of the trip. This huge saltwater crocodile was spotted in this section in the previous days.

We set off and the heat was intense so I remember two of the tourists decided they would cool down and float down the river holding onto their canoe. When we got to the first campsite we looked back at the map and quickly realised the two girls had decided to cool down exactly where the crocodile was last seen. It could have been a costly mistake so they were unbelievably lucky. I didn't take any chances the first day and decided I would wait to cool down later, as I wanted to keep my legs. Each evening we would put up our tents, light a fire and cook some food under the stars. There was a makeshift toilet which consisted of a toilet seat on top of a metal oil drum hidden behind a tree. A track to the toilet from previous groups could be found easily but I still had to tread carefully and I could hear the hiss of the snakes and other creatures in the overgrown grass just inches away. One morning I woke up to find a big Komodo dragon sniffing around the ashes of our campfire looking for food. It didn't seem too interested in us so we didn't get overly excited and it eventually disappeared back into the bushes. I made it back with all limbs intact and no bites after four days and what an adventure it was. It was soon time to pack up and get back on the road. On the last evening in a hostel I decided to watch a movie. This hostel had a little outdoor movie area and they showed different movies each night. So when I sat down alone, a horror movie called 'Wolf Creek' which was based in Australia came on. This movie I purposely avoided watching before travelling. It was a movie based on a true story about backpackers in Australia going missing after breaking down in the outback along their trip. I didn't watch it previously, as I didn't think it would help my nerves while travelling. I thought as I was now half way around

Australia I would stay and watch it. I was a little spooked as to what happened in the movie, especially that it was a true story. I decided to see where in Australia this actually happened. To my complete shock, this area called 'Wolf Creek' was a little too close for comfort to where I was. "Of all places to watch this movie", I thought. I was really glad to be getting back on the road the next day and I just prayed my old car would not break down along the way! This movie did not need a sequel!

It was good to get back on the road and to see a few more places. My plan was to take my time and drive down the east coast which was a very different side of Australia, both literally and in terms of commercialisation. Months went by and life was treating me well but the good times were coming to an end and I would soon have to get back to reality and return home. I always kept in touch with the football results back home and I felt I was really missing out but knew I'd be back soon enough.

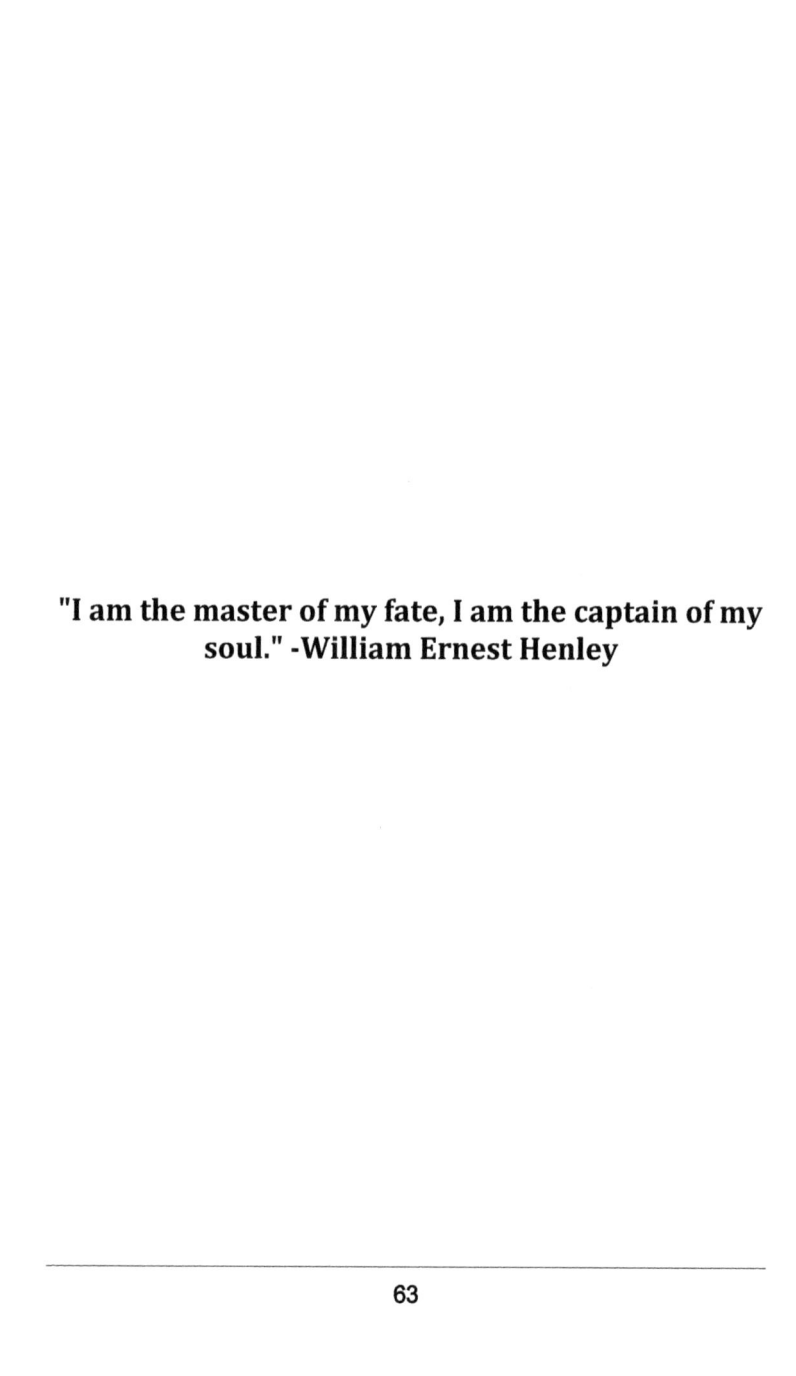

"I am the master of my fate, I am the captain of my soul." -William Ernest Henley

Chapter 9 - Supersize Me

Too much of the good life meant I had put on at least a stone or even two in weight. Football season had just started back home so I needed to work extra hard to shift this weight. It would be hard work so I started even before I flew back home. To make matters worse I was bitten by something the day before I was due to fly out. I was walking home from the cinema on my last night as I didn't fancy being hungover for the mammoth flight home. I was wearing combat shorts and I felt this intense sharp pain on my calf muscle. I thought it was a bad mosquito bite as I slapped my calf with my hand. I looked for what it might have been but I saw nothing. My calf immediately started to swell but I passed it off as most bites swell a little. On the flight home I noticed a small hole was forming in the centre of the swelling where the bite was. The next day the bite was rotting my leg and a hole was forming. I booked an appointment at my local GP's clinic. Lucky enough and by pure chance I got a locum doctor who was from….. Australia and she knew straight away that it was a poisonous spider bite. She said it was a common small poisonous spider which made sense as to why I didn't see it when it bit me. It wasn't life threatening and she put me on antibiotics to clear the inflammation and the wound began to close and heal over the next few weeks.

It was time to get back to playing football. I found my old gear bag, dusted it off and I was raring to go. The break did me good and I was hungrier than ever now but I had a little problem. I was also a different kind of hungry all year so I was overweight with a hole in my leg, and it meant I was not off to the best start to try to impress the new management. The club had changed management during the year while I was away. They gave the job to two outside lads who were both appointed as joint managers. These lads didn't know each other beforehand but would work together in this joint role. One had good credentials as a footballer but the other looked like an accountant and didn't look like a baller, but I thought 'never judge a book by the cover'. I had nothing to fear and I was looking forward to letting them both see me play. My aim was to get my number three jersey back but I knew I had to work hard. I had to put in extra training and worked extra hard to get back into shape. I thought if I got a little sharper, getting back onto the first team wouldn't be too hard. I knew the weight would fall off and the sharpness would come back with some extra work. I never missed training, did the extra work needed after each training but my year away from weekly training took its toll on my body. I was rarely injured up to this but this year it was niggle after niggle. While getting fit I pulled my quad and then I damaged my Achilles tendon. I recovered quick enough as I couldn't afford to miss training and did all that was needed with ice baths and anything to help so I was back quickly each time. This was hard work but I kept plugging away with my sights set on that jersey. Challenge games came and went but I was left on the bench each game. I needed match time to get match sharp but I couldn't get a minute. Even in meaningless challenge games I was left wondering what was going on and what I was doing wrong.

I will never forget one particular game which was under lights one mid week evening. We played a strong senior team from Meath on a cold March evening at a neutral venue. The opposition brought thirty players and at half time they changed the whole team. Fifteen off and fifteen new players on. They wanted to give each squad player time and a chance to show what they had before their league started. They didn't care who won. We had twenty players togged that evening and the new management left the starting fifteen on trying to win this 'hugely important' challenge game. Then with just ten minutes to go our two managers started telling us subs to warm up by calling out names one by one. We had five subs on the bench including me and they called out just four names. Yes, I was left on the bench as winning this challenge game was too important to them to give me a few minutes on the pitch. Going into this game I was actually feeling great and knew I would have played well. I was gutted to be ignored and not worthy of one minute in a challenge game. After the game one of the managers tried to tell me he didn't see me or even know I was there. I didn't bother to even reply to his lies as we both knew the truth. This went on again and again for the whole year. Even in training after the warm up and drills, these guys picked the fifteen players to play backs and forwards and sent the rest up the other end of the pitch to do anything. He even said just go up there and out of the way. Once we didn't get in the way and bother them. I couldn't believe their attitude. At another training, they picked the usual fifteen and said "right the rest of ye Junior B rejects up the other end of the pitch". My self esteem was low but I was confused as to what I was to do to prove myself when I wasn't allowed to play or even really train with the team. I was just written off and not given any opportunity to be even able to show them what I could do. One day I plucked up the courage and I asked one of the managers what I have to do to get some minutes on the pitch and prove myself. I remember he said that everyone will get some time but the truth was he had his favourites and didn't want anyone else involved. I was shocked at his attitude. My chat must have worked, as the very next Sunday morning I was brought on in a challenge game. My name was called to warm up at the beginning of the second half. Some of the crowd were cheering for me as this was my first game since my return. I was brought on to mark a county star forward who was in his prime. It didn't phase me as I had marked many county forwards over the years and I knew I could handle them. My team mate who I replaced, was being destroyed and this star forward was running the show. So how did I do? He went on to score a huge 0-0 on me. Positive? I thought so....not to be. Next game I was overlooked yet again and not even asked to warm up. I thought to myself...what more do I have to do? I think back and I honestly believe he brought me on that day with the hope I would be annihilated by this county star. I would bet he was hoping to embarrass me while proving to himself that I didn't deserve to be near the first team. It backfired on him but he didn't care about my performance that day as he had his team picked and I would never be getting into it even though I just proved that I deserved to be considered.

As the season went on, I spotted that these guys didn't know anything about football so it might not be just me. We had one of the best upcoming talents in our team. He made the breakthrough to senior and was a serious player. He had played County Minor and was a hard hitting, tough back. I remember him getting the nod to warm up in an important game. He came on naturally a little nervous for his senior debut with a decent crowd watching. Within twenty minutes he was hauled off again and subbed. He had made a slight error due to nerves but he was a great player. The damage was done, subbing a player on and off in any game is soul destroying. I could see his head drop and he was broken. After the game he was in bits and being consoled by one of more experienced senior lads. I consoled him and told him not to give up. He said he was quitting football as he had enough. He was crying and nodding his head in dismay as he didn't deserve this but this is how the players were treated in this regime. No manager came up to him afterwards to explain anything. He was just left abandoned to answer his own questions in his head. Lucky for the club he never quit and is now one of the best backs in the club with two senior championship medals to date. These two "managers" almost destroyed this player's career which proves they just "hadn't a breeze"!

Training and games came and went from the rest of the year and yet again I was left out of everything . This management team just wanted to work with the 'first team'. It was clear that I was never going to be part of these lads' plans no matter what I did to prove otherwise. I was going home after both training and games with my confidence and enthusiasm destroyed, wondering what I did wrong to deserve to be treated like an outcast. I wondered what I had done over the space of my year travelling..... to go from a first team player to be treated like dirt. My confidence was low and I was really down in the dumps to no end. I was in constant bad form as nobody had the decency to speak to me and tell me what I needed to do to even get close to the squad. I was unwanted and I didn't know why. Each day I walked into the dressing room with my head hung low and I had lost my sparkle. I used to be laughing and joking in the dressing room but it felt like I shouldn't even be there. After games, I togged in quickly and sometimes didn't bother to hang around to chat. I stopped going for drinks after games as I just didn't feel part of the team any more. It took so much out of me. When I was playing I felt I was representing my town and I did this with such honour. I took such pride in my jersey and enjoyed the after match banter. I walked down the street with my head held high as I was part of the community. But now that I was not playing, nobody put their arm around my shoulder and explained what I was doing wrong or what I could do better. I was just written off and nobody cared but me.

My head was wrecked and it was affecting me so much. As the answers for my team omission were not coming I decided I would go looking for some answers. I was fed up so I spoke to one of the managers again. He indirectly said the reason he wouldn't play me was that he felt that I was overweight. Surprisingly he said he was impressed that I had kept a county man scoreless earlier in the year. I was shocked he actually remembered but there was no point being impressed and not giving me another chance. I hoped this chat would make him think when the next games came around, but it wasn't to be. Any time a player in the backs was injured during a game he would warm up anyone else and use all other available options. One day he even brought on the sub keeper as a forward when there was an injury in the forward line. Most managers would bring on a sub in that position or move an accurate backup as a forward but not these "geniuses". The forwards on the bench were disgusted. I really wanted to quit that day but I loved this game too much to let these two 'muppets' finish my career at only twenty nine years of age. I was worth more than this but it was eating me up inside. That year we won a Division 2 League title but I didn't feel part of the team. I collected my medal at the Christmas Dinner Dance, but deep down I felt like a fraud. I hid at the back for the team photo. I didn't even tog out for that last game of the year as I knew I was not in their plans. I don't count that medal in my medal haul and looking back I probably shouldn't have even accepted it. championships came and we never progressed. One of managers took off to the sun on his summer holidays and missed most of the championship so these guys were a shambles, winning a Division 2 League or not. Lucky enough for the future of the club, both these managers left and went their merry way that winter... "sayonara to these two lads"! I felt so relieved as I knew that a change was coming which meant I could get a fresh chance with a new manager. It really shows how toxic an influence a poor manager(s) can have on a club's future. So many players can walk away when a manager's ego is bigger than the club.

I already had to set my sights on the next season and I would do everything in my power to get fit, lose weight and give whoever the new manager was, no option but to have me on their minds when picking the team. Whether I was a sub or starter, I just wanted to be involved every weekend. In the off season, things didn't start too well. I was so run down, I contracted the mumps. I was wiped of energy and would be out of action for weeks. How did I get the mumps? I was working in a big company and many of us GAA lads used to meet for our breaks and talk football. One guy was from a neighbouring club and he was very dramatic and animated in his storytelling. I remember him telling a story and could see the spit flying across the table where I was. Little did I know he was getting over the mumps and he was still contagious! A few days later I went downhill, my energy gone along with swollen glands in my neck. I didn't mind once I didn't get the mumps down below. I had always wanted children and I heard mumps can stop this from happening. I was totally drained all day and recovery was very slow. I was eager and just wanted to get fit again but I was too eager and came back to training too soon and relapsed.

One morning I woke up in a lot of discomfort. I tried to get dressed and I found it hard to put on my jeans. My right testicle had become inflamed and eventually was the size of my fist. Thoughts of not being able to become a father took over my mind. I jumped into the car and drove down to the doctor on call in my local hospital. Driving was very uncomfortable as the swelling was so big. After seeing the doctor, I was booked in for more tests and further scans. I arrived at the hospital for a scan shortly after. They wanted to do a few scans to rule out testicular cancer. I remember being told to put on the hospital robe and to lie on a table. A machine was brought in and I was gelled up below to scan my enormous testicle. At one stage during this scan, I had three nurses standing there examining my oversized testicle using an ultrasound machine. They were chatting to see what was wrong and making sure it wasn't anything else untoward. While the nurses were having a big discussion, I was lying there thinking there are not many times in life where you would have three women examining and discussing your balls! I also thought that it would make a great photo to send to my friends but then nobody would want to see that! Luckily enough, all the test results came back clear and there was nothing else to worry about. They just put it down to the mumps and off I waddled home, with most of my dignity still intact. When the swelling eventually went down I noticed things did not look or feel the same as before. I booked a GP visit and I was told, after a quick check, that I was now down to one working testicle below. The mumps had taken out one of my engines. It was like flying in a plane and I now had to rely on the one engine to get me through my journey. Let's hope the one working one I had left was a strong 'Rolls Royce' one. The mumps had caused one of my testicles to shrink which is called testicular atrophy. I knew that some men who have had mumps can become sterile which was a huge worry. I was only recently married and I always wanted children so only time would tell. I thought back to the lunch I had with the guy who had the mumps and I wondered why someone who was contagious would come to work and spread it. Why did I sit across from him? But then I didn't know anything about mumps at the time. Hindsight is a great thing and the damage was done. Time to get on with it and hope I could still have children.

"There's always a tomorrow and the hope of something new." - Helen Steiner Rice

Chapter 10 - New Manager - New Hope

A new year brought the announcement of the new team manager. As you can imagine, I was particularly delighted. It was even better news as the new manager was a former club player….. and it gets better. He managed the team many years earlier when I was in my early 20's, flying fit and he always started me. He usually started me at wing back or centre back and I knew he liked me as a player, as he liked players who went in hard. I was glad to see him back and it was a new chance for me to get on to the team. It was nearly ten years since he was last in charge so I wasn't just as nimble but I had worked extra hard on losing the extra Oz weight. I was finally getting into shape after a few minor setbacks. Training was going well and there were plenty of challenge games booked in for preseason. I was confident of getting some game time as I was going well in training. In one of the first challenge games we were playing at home. The visiting team had loads of injury problems and their manager announced that they only brought thirteen players. They knew they had little chance against us after bringing so few players, especially with no subs and we had a decent sized squad.

Instead of calling the game off both managers agreed to play, as a competitive game is always better than a training session. I had a recurring back injury but never told anyone and I just togged out as always hoping to play. I knew I needed game time so I didn't care. Both managers decided to play fifteen aside so it meant the other team taking two players from our squad to make up the fifteen. There is embarrassment to whoever would get picked as it shows you may not be in the manager's plans. So you guessed it....myself and another young lad were told to tog out for the visiting team. I looked around the dressing room and got a few jeers but it didn't bother me. This was a first for me but I knew I was better than some of the players left in the fifteen. But once I was getting to play I was happy. I was guaranteed to get sixty minutes of football and that's all I thought about. Deep down I was actually kind of happy he chose me to play for the opposition. It sort of felt like a game of poker, where our manager thought he had a great hand. He was overconfident and little did he know he just gave away two aces. He gave away two players without thinking. I knew what I could do on the pitch so I was excited. I knew I would prove him wrong but now was my time to show it. My position on the pitch was in the backs but the opposition manager said he was missing a few forwards, so he asked us both to play as forwards. I was given the number ten jersey, my former county jersey for Cavan. I thought back to my younger days playing on the wing. My other team mate was put in at full forward and given the number fourteen jersey. In my opinion he was a great footballer so I was surprised he was given to the opposition, but then it may have shown that our manager made a rash decision picking the two players to give away. We took up our positions on the pitch and I was quite happy to find myself marking a lad that I knew I was better than. Inside I knew I should be wearing my own club colours but I had nothing to lose and I would be giving it my all. It wasn't long before I scored a goal and I heard my own club manager calling me a traitor from the sideline. The handy win he was expecting against thirteen lads plus us two loanees wasn't so handy now. It wasn't too long before myself and my teammate who were sent to help the opposition notched up 1-6 between us against our own club. We both linked up so well and all our scores were assisted by the other. I kicked 1-3 and he scored 0-3. As the game was drawing to a close it was nip and tuck and nothing between the sides. The game ended as a draw with a last minute free kick from the homeside but you could see that it felt like a loss. Inside I was delighted as it showed yet again the amount of belief the management had in my ability. Maybe it would make them start to think about me again. Little did I know being called a traitor would surface again in the future. I was pleased with my performance as I tried my best and thought I did ok but of course, there's always room for improvement.

The following weekend came and we had a league game. As expected I started on the bench alongside my teammate who I had scored 1-3 on the week before in the challenge game. With fifteen minutes to go in the game, the manager called a few subs to warm up. Who got called? Me? No, but my team mate who I had just scored 1-3 on only the week before. I was left on the bench yet again and didn't get a minute. I just didn't understand but I kept my head down and of course blamed myself for not being good enough. I thought that maybe I am actually useless and just need to accept it. Maybe I need to hang up my boots, as this is telling me that I have no chance to break into the team. I have tried again and again and got nowhere. Some managers just do not know the impact their decisions have on players' mental health, especially when football means so much to some players. Players with low self confidence get such a boost with any praise and when they play well the praise flows. Sometimes they don't get much praise at home so this is the only boost to their confidence they may get. When players get ignored and left out it reminds them of rejection.

I loved playing too much so I never gave up. The only way I would know for sure if it was my ability that was in question, was to play well for our second team, the good auld Junior B's. The only problem was that we were struggling with numbers to field a second team and the management were conceding games every weekend. Some weekends we would have twelve unused fresh players togged and ready to take the field. We just needed three lads to stay togged from the first team. When I played for the first team I always made myself available to help the second team, so this was a normal thing to do. Unfortunately this senior manager didn't want these players to be over tired. This meant the reserve players were left with no games week after week. The championship was getting closer with time running out to try to prove myself. Each week the decision to concede games wasn't ever given much thought. Little did they realise it meant so much to me and I am sure many others who were trying to break into the first team. It was so frustrating. Sometimes I wonder if the games were conceded just so the manager could get to the pub quicker to watch the football on Super Sunday.

That year, I captained the Junior B team. The championship arrived and we won the first away game. We had just beaten one of the favourite teams in the opening match, so it was a great start. I was back playing at full back and I had my favourite number 3 jersey. I played a good enough game but I would always find minor faults with my game where I needed to improve. Our supporters were great and they told me after some games that I was "outstanding". I am my own worst critic and I appreciated the nice comments, but it didn't go to my head. I just did my job and my focus was to get back on the first team. I could read the game quite well and I knew where to be during the game. I read my player and I knew after the first ball if I needed to play slightly ahead of him or alongside him. I knew I needed consistent, good performances with the second team. I knew the senior manager had to be watching so I hoped this might help my chances to be considered again. With the senior championship fast approaching I was happy that I was finally getting fit and playing well. It felt good and my confidence was improving with each game. The supporters wouldn't be long letting you know otherwise…. and the praise continued.

With time quickly running out and with just one league game to go before the senior championship began. There was a double header away to a club. This was against the team I made my senior debut many years before. This was always my target game to be seen and hopefully to do everything I could to make a statement. The senior team took to the field first. Thoughts were going through my head "just play out of your skin in the next game and he will have to consider you for next week". The senior game finished and it was the second team up next. We had a full dressing room. The junior manager was on his holidays so the senior manager was in charge. Just about to take the field and word came in that we conceded the junior game as we didn't want to risk players with The senior championship coming up. I was gutted and so disappointed. I knew this was my last chance to prove a point. My senior chances were dashed! I trained again the following week but I knew the team and subs were picked. A week later the seniors were knocked out of the championship. Season over for everyone.

"If you don't make a decision then time will make it for you and time will always side against you!"
- Billy Graham

Chapter 11 - Decision Time

I was now thirty-one years old and I hadn't played first team football in three seasons. I knew I had something to offer but I was left abandoned and sitting on a shelf. Most players in my situation would have just quit. Lots of players don't even make it to the age of thirty-one. During the off season it was time for me to do some serious thinking. I had moved house and I found myself living in the next parish over. This was minutes from my own club but they had a very good junior team. This team had made three Junior county finals in three years but they just couldn't seem to get over the line. I went to watch them in the third county final, having moved to the area. I said to myself before the game, that if they lost this final, I would do my best to help them win one and transfer to them. I had just taken a huge mental step by even thinking I would do this. This is a massive decision in football, as transferring between clubs isn't very common and frowned upon by many. I just felt so wasted sitting on a bench and not playing any football, especially when I felt I could still offer something. Leaving your club is not something you do lightly but I was glad I was starting to see a way that I could play more football.

The championship final started and after just five minutes the star forward for the team I was shouting for was taken out of it. He was clean through on goal and out of nowhere a kamikaze pilot hit him from the side and he slammed into the grass with a bounce. It looked very nasty. It was like a steam train milling through a car at an intersection. I can still hear the shattering impact. It was probably the worst and most blatant tackle I have ever witnessed on a GAA pitch. This player clearly was given a job to do and boy did he do it in style. He just took out the main attacking threat and it didn't look good for the target. The referee stopped the game as there was no movement from the star forward. The two men were down but there was some movement from the kamikaze pilot. He injured himself so he left the field but his mission was accomplished. Even in a rugby game it would be deemed a dangerous tackle and a red card but the referee went to his pocket and produced a yellow card. The crowd were disgusted. The target player was lifted to his feet after he came around. He refused a stretcher and he stumbled in a daze all the way past us in the stand and into the dressing room. His eyes in a fixed stare, his legs rubbery, his jaw hung low and a trickle of blood dripped down his face. He was brought straight to the hospital and it later emerged he had a broken jaw, broken collar bone and a bad concussion. It was not a pleasant incident to witness and the fact that a mere yellow card was shown to the out of control juggernaut was such a disgrace. The game continued but it was so evident that losing this key forward was the difference. Unfortunately, it was third time unlucky for this team as they went on to lose yet again by the smallest of margins. It was quite clear that if the main target man was on the field, they would have won this elusive title. Keeping to tradition, both winning and losing teams went back to a local hotel for dinner - the hotel in question was the main sponsor. As you can imagine there were two extremes in the function room. One team singing and roaring with the cup held high and the other team hoping the dinner comes quickly so they can eat it quickly and run. Just as the lads were finishing their dinner and ready to go, the kamikaze pilot entered the room after a quick visit to the hospital. The winning team stood and went into raptures and gave him a hero's welcome into the function room. He had completed his mission and he had won them the championship! Meanwhile the losing full forward was spending the night in hospital with broken bones and concussion. The losing team immediately got up, left their half eaten dinners and hit for home, feeling totally dejected and robbed. Their faces now rubbed into what was a shocking and obvious tactic that won a championship at the expense of almost killing the best player on the pitch.

That night I joined the lads for a few pints to drown their sorrows. It was like they read my mind as a few of them asked me to transfer across and join them for the following season. I smirked and nodded at the compliment but I kept my cards close to my chest. They said it would make sense to transfer as I was living there now and they knew that I wasn't playing any football. It was decision time, but I think I had made a decision in my head earlier. I mulled it over for the rest of the winter but deadline day was fast approaching. I found the transfer form online, filled it out and I kept it in my car. I sometimes even carried it around with me in case I bumped into the club chairman or secretary. No time ever felt like the right time to leave as my club was in my heart and I had played for this club for 25 years. To make myself feel better I told myself that I was not *leaving* them, I was just no longer wanted or was surplus to requirements. Even then it was still such a big decision for me. I drove by the secretary and chairperson's houses many times and I bottled it every time. One day while out cutting sticks for a club timber sale, I had the transfer request in my back pocket. I tried to find the right time to hand it over. It was like trying to tell someone that they owed me money or that I was looking for time off work. I expected a negative reaction and I hated conflict. No time seemed right so another day went by. As the deadline for transfers was now days away my hand was forced into action. I gathered the courage and I made the very long two minute drive over to the club secretary's house with my slip of paper in my pocket. To her shock I told her I was requesting a transfer.

The silence said it all. In a small community, word got out quickly and texts were coming in asking if it was true. I received a few phone calls to say a few of the committee were going to meet with me to have a chat with me to ask me to reconsider, as no club wants to lose a player. When these meetings never took place it was quite clear I wasn't too important or wanted. One night I was out for a pint and I was chatting to the club chairman at the time. He said he would approve the move and wished me the best of luck. This was great as I knew it was going to happen now. He was an excellent footballer whom I respected so I was delighted that he genuinely wished me well. Some of the lads were happy for me and said I was 100% right as I was leaving to play some ball but others remained silent which can only mean one thing. I remember the chairman saying that the new club I was going to was a decent team and that I might not make the first team. I told him thanks for his concerns but that was only up to me and not for him to worry about. I shook his hand and appreciated his opinion and advice. So just like that, twenty-five years at the club I loved was finished and that was it. It was all over, no pats on the back, no thanks for the commitment but this is the way I would have preferred to have gone out - with no fuss. It was now up to me to prove everyone wrong. I didn't have to prove anything to myself as I still had the belief that I could bring something to a team if I was allowed to play.

"Remember the guy that gave up? Neither does anybody else!" - Anonymous

Chapter 12 - Fresh Beginnings

Shortly after Christmas my new club held their first team meeting. I was nervous as I really didn't know what to expect. When I walked into the meeting room all the chairs were laid out in rows with five chairs in each row. The top table had four seats facing the players. I was warmly welcomed by my new teammates. When I looked up at the top table I was immediately put at ease. A familiar face was smiling back at me. Sitting at the top table was a retired player from my old club. He was on the team when I won my first Junior B championship medal. Back then I was starting my football career and he was finishing his. He was a key player when he won a senior championship back in 1992 and he was a very cool and calm footballer. He was a great reader of the game and like myself, he appreciated a physical battle. To my delight this man was going to be my new manager at my new club. He told me from that day that he had big plans for me in the team and that I would be either starting centre back or midfield. The lift in confidence he immediately gave me was just immense. To be thought of so highly after all the years being treated so badly by previous managers. Going from not getting a jersey and being left out of match day squads to being told I was going to be starting in central positions. I had forgotten what it felt like to be excited about football again. He instantly boosted my confidence and I wanted to repay him on the football field. I was now being given some respect which was the polar opposite of the last few years. It was weird for me starting with a new team at thirty-one years of age and having to leave all my club mates and best friends behind me. But as I said all along, I just wanted to play football. This club seemed exactly what I needed. I knew they would get the best out of me if my confidence came back. As the meeting drew to a close, we set a goal for the year and we were all up for the battle that lay ahead. Winning the championship was the goal and everyone believed we could achieve this after being so close so many times in the previous years. It was all positive but the talking needed to be done on the pitch.

Preseason started and we played a few friendly games. The second friendly game was announced which was going to be against my old club! That day I woke up nervous as I had to go back to my old club and tog out in the away dressing room. It was only a few months since I was in the home dressing room. All eyes were on me. It was preseason and I knew that I wasn't fit but not many were. I wanted to show that I was still a half decent player. Not only showing my new club but I was still trying to prove myself to my old club for some reason. As the game started I immediately intercepted the first ball that was kicked towards my man. I started to make a driving solo run from the half back line to the half forward line like a bullet. I could hear my ex teammate behind me, half in shock and wondering why he wasn't catching up with me. I gave a one-two and on the return I hurried a shot for a point but I put it wide. I jogged back to my half back position but I was shattered after my big burst..... but I couldn't show it. I think the adrenalin made me make such a daring run. My ex teammate was still wondering what had just happened, as did I. As the game went on, it was hard to get stuck into my old teammates. I pulled out of so many tackles that I normally wouldn't. I usually go into a tackle and take no prisoners but maybe I had too much love and respect for my old team. I also didn't want to injure anyone, especially my friends in a preseason challenge game.

It wasn't long before March crept up, which meant it was the start of the league campaign. I was starting at full back. It was a home game and I noticed a few of my old teammates had come to watch me play. I wasn't sure if they wanted to see me play well or if they were there to ensure the transfer was a right thing to do for my old club. I never knew the truth but I had to try to move on and not care what others thought of my decision to move. I didn't play particularly well that day as my fitness and match sharpness weren't there yet. My manager knew it was early in the season and he always focussed on the positives. He had such faith in me that I would be flying fit come the championship. He had no doubts at all and I fed off his positive beliefs. As the season went on, it wasn't long before word got back that I wasn't playing anything special with my new club. Some people were relieved that it wasn't a mistake to sanction the transfer.

As the season progressed I played at either centre back or midfield. The last time I played in midfield, it was at underage level so this was new to me again. The manager usually started me at number eight and I began to form a solid partnership in midfield with a 'proper' midfielder. I was the holding man, which suited me, as I wouldn't have the legs. My midfield partner had a great set of hands and an engine that would run all day. The club were desperate to lift that championship cup and they were close so many times. Their last championship was 1994 and the whole parish was desperate to get their hands on it again. That year the championship draw was made and we were drawn against an old rival. They were a very up and coming young team and one of the favourites this year. The teams had met a few times in the past and it was always fairly even. It was usually a very close game with the narrowest of margins between the sides at the end of each game. I was looking forward to my championship debut with my new club. Championship is what it is all about! Training was going very well and our team just couldn't wait to get to match day. When the day finally came around, the two teams arrived but both had the same coloured jerseys. Lucky enough they had a second kit so we got to play in our colours. We played pretty badly that day. I wasn't impressed with my own performance either. We equalised with a last minute point so a replay was on the cards to decide who would progress to the next round. We got out of jail that day. We now had one week to try to re-focus ourselves and we knew we could play so much better.

The replay came around and it was now our turn to wear an away kit but we didn't have an away kit at the time. A kit bag appeared in the dressing room. One of the selectors opened the bag and out came my old club's jerseys. Wow, what were the chances! I had tried for years to get to put back on my club's jersey and now I was lined out at centre half back and got to put on the number six. It felt good as this was probably my favourite position when I played for my old club even though I usually played at full back. For some reason or another, everything went right for me that day. Every ball I went for ended up in my hands. Every pass I kicked went to the chest of my teammate and every tackle was well timed, which wasn't like me at all. I seemed to have energy to run all day. Maybe it was down to my old jersey. We played so much better that day and when the final whistle came we won and we had just knocked out one of the favourite teams. We would be in the pot for the quarter finals and it felt so good. That feeling of elation at the final whistle is something very special. This was a feeling I had not felt in such a long time. Winning while watching a game from the sidelines is nowhere near the feeling of winning where you are really involved in the win. It was kind of ironic that day where I won while wearing my old club's jersey.... and wearing a number I would have loved to have worn for my old club. I was picked as 'Man of the Match' after our championship win and word slowly got around that I played well. I still didn't care what people thought but I was just happy to have played sixty minutes and contributed towards a good win for my new team.

Life on the pitch was beginning to go well again but I started to find more and more bitter people around me. Everywhere I went I was called a traitor. Around the same time, another big name county player had moved counties to represent another county and it hadn't gone down well at all. So the 'traitor tag' was being used regularly. I was hearing all the sly and nasty comments in the pub. "One Life One Club" was said loudly as I was chatting in company. "Traitor" followed by a laugh and "I'm only messing". I still find it funny that if you transfer out of your club you can be called a traitor but if you have players who transfer into your club you are not a traitor. My old club had a player who transferred in to them who was part of a legendary team that went on to win a senior championship in 1992 but he was always known as a legend. There was never a mention of his transfer or the word 'traitor'. He transferred from his home club, so which is it?

The quarter final game came round but we never "showed up" on an awful wet day. None of us played well. Unfortunately we were knocked out and the season was abruptly over. This was not the plan but we had to take it on the chin and dust ourselves off. I knew we weren't too far off and I already started to think about the next season. After the game we went for a few drinks. If we ever had a bad defeat, supporters and players from other clubs would make an obvious bee line for me in the pub to ask me how things were going with the new club and what the score was from the defeat. When we won and I played well, they stayed away. I knew they were hoping that I would say that I was not getting a game. When I told them that I was making the team it was not the answer they wanted. They would dig deeper and want to know what position I played in. When I told them I was playing either midfield or centre back, you could hear the word getting around like it was a joke. The bitterness and nastiness was eye opening. Some nights I would just want a quiet pint and old retired club players would ask me what was the difference in winning a Junior A or a Junior B medal. In other words if you stayed you could have won a Junior B medal with my old club. They knew that Junior A is first team football and that Junior B is second team football but they just wanted to get a dig in for me leaving the club. I didn't need to explain to these lads that the fact that I was not getting any games was the reason I left. They would have known this if they went to watch the games but it was just easier to jump on the bandwagon and criticise me. I knew they were just bitter that I left in the first place and while I had no regrets, I was disappointed with some people's attitudes towards my transfer. I really just wanted to be able to actually play football for my last few years. After a while I stopped going out to the pub. I couldn't go to any of my locals as inevitably football chat would come up and as the drinks went down the abuse would come out..... so many nasty and negative people who hated to hear of anyone doing too well with another club. I wouldn't mind but some of these more vocal lads never kicked a ball in their lives or if they did, they packed it in at seventeen to drink and smoke and they never gave any proper commitment to their clubs. They just didn't have the heart that I had and were just too lazy, in my opinion. To me they had no real pride in their own clubs when they couldn't even be bothered playing when they had the ability to do so. They were the real traitors.

"Timing is everything. If it's meant to happen it will, at the right time for the right reasons."
- Unknown

Chapter 13 - Timing is Key

As a team, things didn't really go as we had planned in my first year at my new club. We didn't get promoted in the league and we got knocked out in the quarter finals of the championship. My ex teammate and manager decided to step down and left that winter due to work commitments. The assistant manager took over the reins. He had won a championship with the club in 1994 and he was a key player at the time. In the past he had played with Cavan so had good knowledge and experience. He was football mad and loved his club with the clubs colours pumping through his veins. He was very passionate and practically spent most of his days at the pitch or in the clubhouse. He was a man who liked the physicality of the game so he liked my style. When the league started we got off to a great start. We won the first few games and we were in a healthy position but as the games came thick and fast we slipped up mid season. We found ourselves dropping down the league table rapidly. championship was now approaching and with only one week to go before the first round, the County Board sprang a rescheduled league game on us. I had thoughts of someone getting injured and with a small squad this was massive. We couldn't risk losing anyone but we had to play this game. It seemed crazy to squeeze a game in……. and to make matters worse we were playing the top team. The outcome of this game was huge for us, as we needed a single point to secure division two status for the following year. We started the game well and we were matching them in all areas of the pitch. I was holding my own playing in midfield. Then with just twenty minutes to go, the opposition broke at speed and they were running at pace towards our goal. There was one free man not being tracked at all. I had to make a challenge as he was going to get a score. As I ran towards him, he side stepped me so I decided I would take a card for the team and I left my leg in to foul him and stop him progressing.

Looking back it was a mad tackle. He was running at speed and he ploughed through me but my body didn't budge. He twisted my outstretched leg like a turnstile. I spun and hit the floor. The pain hit me and it was excruciating. The sudden surge of pain meant I didn't know if my leg was broken, facing sideways or hacked clean off. I couldn't feel my leg and I was face down in the warm grass afraid to look at the damage. I opened my eyes but it was just darkness. I couldn't actually lift my head with the pain I was in but I heard some commotion around me. I could hear the voice of our chairman, who doubled as the team physio. I could feel him beside me and he asked me if I was ok. I turned my head, took a deep breath and opened my eyes. I sat up and he gave me some water. "Think we will need more than water for this one", I said with a grimace. I took my yellow card from the referee, as I expected. I was helped to my feet and I slowly walked off while waving at the manager to bring a sub on for a while. I sat in the dugout flexing my knee. I knew something was still not right even though the pain had stopped. The game was very close with just five minutes to go. All the players were starting to tire around the pitch. The manager looked to the bench and told me to get warmed up again as he needed me back in for the last five minutes. I was tempted but I told him I couldn't as something wasn't right. I knew he was half pissed off but he knew if I could have played that I would have. The last few minutes felt like half an hour but the ref finally blew his whistle and we had held out for the important point which was enough to survive and remain in Division 2. A huge result for us!

We had the team huddle on the pitch and then the warm down. I joined in the warm down but my knee kept buckling under me. In the showers the same, my knee kept giving way and I almost fell a few times so I knew something was wrong. I drove home and spent the evening testing and flexing my knee. It was feeling ok but it was just so weak when I walked on it.

Deep down I knew something was wrong but I tried to convince myself that it was just a small injury or a slight tear. The next morning I booked an appointment with my local physio to see what the damage was. He squeezed me in that day as I told him it was urgent. I sat up on the table and he got me to flex my knee and he moved my kneecap about. He knew from the tears in my eyes how much I didn't want him to say that it was bad news so he didn't give it to me. He told me it would be better to get an MRI and it may be nothing. I got a huge lift from this even though I knew that he was trying to give me some hope. Later that day I phoned for an MRI and I got a cancellation for 6.30am the next morning in Santry. I wanted to have a chance of getting the results back that same day and was glad I got the first appointment that morning. After the MRI they told me that it can take up to 48 hours to get the results back. I asked if there was any chance that I could get them that evening as it was now only 8am. They knew by my face that I really needed to know, so they kindly agreed to get the results out that evening, before close of business. I just couldn't wait and I had to find out if I was ok and could play some part in the upcoming championship game. I also knew the manager would be ringing me and asking me what the damage was. Throughout the day while I was waiting for the results, I was thinking of different ways that I could still play in the championship. Maybe I could strap my knee up or get an injection to numb the pain before the game. After my drive back home, I waited for a couple of long hours before I rang my local GP. I asked the secretary if my MRI results were in and they had just landed. I took a deep breath, crossed my fingers and prayed for good news as the results were being looked at. Unfortunately for me it was the worst news I could have hoped for. I had torn three ligaments in my knee including the big one, the dreaded Anterior Cruciate Ligament (ACL). I thanked the secretary, hung up the phone, put my hands on my head and burst into tears. I was gutted. I couldn't talk to anyone for the day. My manager rang that evening and I told him the news. He was so mad and he gave out to me about my crazy tackle. He didn't mean it personally but he was thinking about the team. The tears came again as I was so annoyed with myself so I hung up the phone. I let him and the team down. Why did I go into such a stupid tackle? What if I hadn't? This can't be the end of my career, can it?

Championship day arrived and it was so strange for me to not have to get my gear ready, eat the right foods, drink extra water etc. Stuff you probably should do every day but on a match day everything was planned. Walking into Breffni Park dressing rooms felt odd for me as I wasn't togging out. I was hobbling around at a loose end trying to keep busy but I didn't know what to do. I should have been togging out but instead I was handing out bibs whilst trying to hold back my tears. I just wanted to be part of the team and play. I did my best to help with the warm up but I really wanted to be on the pitch. This was hard to stomach and the thoughts of that stupid tackle came back again and again. I stood for the team photo in my tracksuit but I really wanted to be wearing a jersey. The squad was hit with more injuries just before the game and as the squad was already small, every player injured was a huge loss. We played very poorly that day and we lost narrowly. There was a new format that year which meant every club had another chance to get through. It was a must win game or that was it, season over. There was no time between games and with players still not back from injury, we lost again and our championship was over for another year. The dressing room was silent. I was gutted! I felt partly to blame as I could have helped if I didn't get myself injured. I am not saying the result would have been any different if I was playing but I would have tried my best.

Over the next few weeks I went back to my physio, and he said not to worry that I will be back in no time. I really needed this positivity as I wasn't feeling very positive. I didn't want to think my footballing days could be over in the way it happened. I got a huge boost from these comments. On the way out the door I met an old school friend who played for another local club. As you do at a local physio, we compared injuries and I told him my bad news. I remember his sincerity when he said "Niall you're finished, 100%". He said that he guaranteed me that I would never play again as he said that he did his cruciate when he was flying fit at twenty odd years old and found it hard to get back. I was now thirty four years old! Not a hope he said over and over again. Each time he said it, it was like getting a punch in the gut. He said that at my age your career is gone. I smiled and told him that time would tell, but on the inside I was thinking maybe he was right. My heart sank at that thought. I had let him get into my head. Football was everything to me but I didn't want to watch football from the sidelines. I wanted to play for another few years. It couldn't all end here as I hadn't fulfilled my promise to my new club. I sat in my car with the realisation that my playing days might be over. I still had some fire inside me and I didn't feel I was ready to stop. I knew I could get back from this injury and play again.

"Winners never quit and quitters never win."

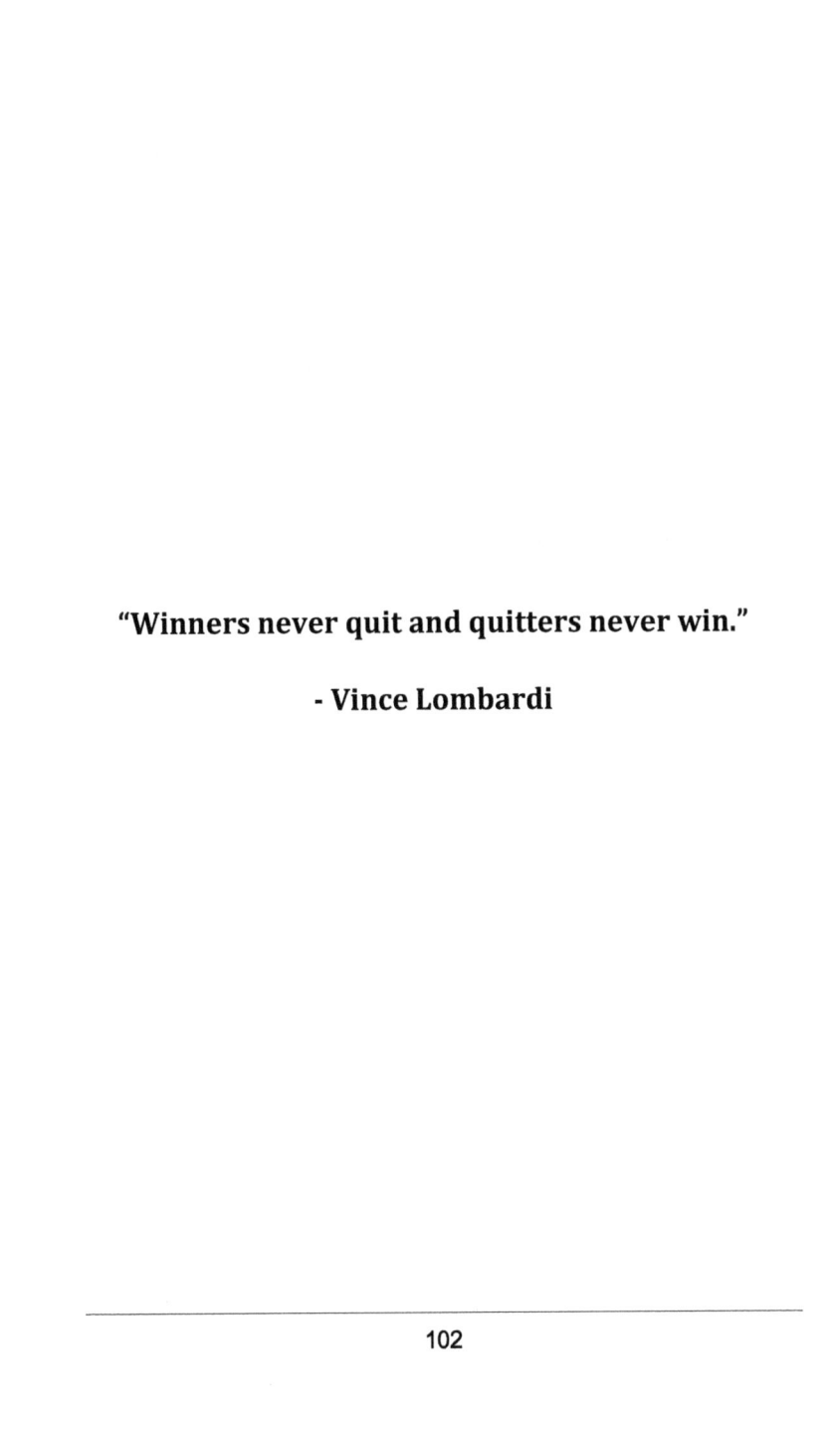

- Vince Lombardi

Chapter 14 – The Road to Recovery

After the swelling in my knee went down it was time for my cruciate operation. I was booked in for early October so this meant that I had all winter and preseason to get my knee strengthened up. I knew the league would be starting in Spring so I knew I could aim to be back playing around mid season. The weekend before the operation I had a stag in Kilkenny with a gang of old friends. As you do with a bunch of lads from different clubs, football chat came up. After a good few drinks my injury was brought up and yet again I was told that I was finished as I was too old. I could not recover to play again at my age was the general consensus. I wasn't only just told, I was guaranteed 100% that I would not come back from this injury. "Not a hope" people commented. As the drinks went in the negativity was everywhere. Not one person gave me any hope and I remember bursting into tears at the bar. It hit me that my football career could suddenly be over but I wasn't ready to say goodbye. I always thought I could play better, do more, and win more. I wasn't ready to finish but maybe these people were right. They all had played football and some of them had this operation before and found it difficult to come back so it forced them to pack it in. These lads were much younger than me and they gave me zero hope. They drained all the positivity that I had and I was now so deflated. Maybe it was time to see sense and just focus on being able to play with my kids without limping. Maybe it was actually time to hang up the auld boots. I dried up the tears, recomposed myself and made the most of the rest of the night.

When I got back to the hotel there were a few lads in the residents bar so I joined them for a night cap. To my delight again, I was then attacked by another member of the stag for being "a traitor". Typically this was from a young local lad who never kicked a ball for his club at senior level. He may have played some under age but he never committed. He questioned my loyalty to the club and he himself was another one who was too lazy to train or tog out for his club. I was sick of people questioning my loyalties and them knowing nothing about me. I was fed up with people talking badly about me for something I loved to do. I was one of very few players to continue playing football nearly into his thirties from my under age footballing days. Loyalty!! To me loyalty is sacrificing your life for your club for twenty five or so years. I was hobbling around with sore limbs, a bad back, bent fingers and these were now my mementos of good hits and games and not complaints about something I loved to do. It was now 4am, and my loyalty was being attacked by someone who had none as he didn't give up his time for the club. My blood boiled that night. I took a deep breath, I got up, left my drink at the bar and went to my room. I still regret that I didn't tell him what I thought of his loyalty. I couldn't wait to get back home so I could get away from the negativity.

"It's hard to beat a person who never gives up." - Babe Ruth

Chapter 15 - Was this the End?

It was now the day for my cruciate ligament reconstruction surgery. I visited Santry early that morning and I met my surgeon. He outlined the procedure and I knew that I was in very safe hands. He was a top surgeon and regarded the best in the country and an ACL specialist. I got into my surgical gown and wheeled into the operating theatre. I met the surgeon in his scrubs and he introduced me to his team. The anaesthetist told me what he was doing and mid sentence I was knocked out. I woke up after the operation and I was lying on a bed in a different room. I was told by the nurse that the operation went perfectly and that it was a very successful reconstruction. Part of the procedure was an overnight stay at this top clinic. I was on morphine for the pain but I felt fine. As it was a Saturday, it meant loads of soccer on TV and I had my own flat screen TV attached to the bed. It was a day watching football for me and some food was delivered to my bed that evening so I was happy out. It was like a hotel. I slept like a baby that night and early the next morning I got out of bed and hopped into the shower. I was ready for my first stroll with my assigned physio on my new cool red crutches. I had never used crutches before but I seemed to take to them ok. The surgeon visited me later that morning and he was very happy with everything so I was discharged. I was given my daily exercise to do which started that day. I knew the more I did the quicker I would be back so I was going to do whatever it took. They would be seeing me again throughout the recovery to ensure all was going ok.

I was collected that afternoon to start the recuperation but not before a quick trip to IKEA. IKEA on crutches is not advisable. I hobbled around but it wasn't long before I got the sweats from the morphine wearing off. I had to find the nearest exit from this maze before I collapsed. Lucky for me, I found a lift and I was out. I felt relieved to get out of there alive as I was starting to panic when it got so crowded.

The daily exercises were very gradual. I started them as soon as I got back home. I pictured the faces of all the people who told me my career was over. I could hear these lads saying "YOU WILL NEVER KICK A BALL AGAIN" "YOU ARE FINISHED". I pictured the guy at the physio waiting room and the guy on the stag. They didn't know how committed I was to getting back on the pitch. I constantly said to myself "I will be back playing". A few days after the operation, the team were training at the pitch. I hopped into my car and drove down to watch them. I walked over to the sideline where the manager was. He approached me and he asked me when I was having my operation. He was still annoyed with me for getting injured. So without looking at him I told him that I had it on Saturday just gone. I could see him stop and stare at me with his mouth open. He said "what.....Saturday....like three days ago.....where are your crutches?" I said I didn't need them and that I could manage without them. He was half shocked and half wondering if I was winding him up. I told him I would be back in six months or so and that I had already started my recovery. He looked stunned and lost for words, which was not like him at all as he always was quick with a response.

Everyday exercise was vital to get movement into my knee. On the days I found motivation hard to come by, I pictured myself playing again. This would force me to get up and do my routine. The shiny new red crutches were left in the corner of the sitting room and my kids played with them. The stairs were the only tricky obstacle in the house. Going up and down was tough going for me at the beginning, but if it was tough it meant it would help strengthen my knee. So I went up and down as much as I could. Firstly, I would do this on my own and then I would add some weights, so I carried my baby son Finn on my back. As I got stronger I did it with daughter Ava too, who was now three years old. They loved being part of my exercise routine. I could feel the burn in my knee but I knew it was getting stronger everyday. Naturally I had my bad days where I found it hard to get out of bed to start my routine, but all I had to do was think of getting onto the field again and up I would get. I continued going to visit my physio every week and stepped up the training all the time with a focus on football the following season. At every visit I asked my physio when would I be back and if I was on track. He always smiled and said that everyone's recovery is different but he always kept me positive by telling me that I would be back when I was ready. He always told me he never had any doubts about me playing football again. I knew he sensed my worst fear, which was not being able to play football again. After many visits and after lots of recovery work, he told me that my quad had gained serious mass and strength. He could see I was putting in serious work. After four months of recovery and exercises I went back for a routine visit to the surgeon in Santry. During my strength assessment my left leg after the operation was now 97% as strong as my right leg. This sounded great to me and once I was making progress I was happy. The surgeon said it looked great and he could see muscle definition. He could see I had done serious training to have it so strong. He told me that my recovery would have me back on track after 6/7 months from the operation date. This meant that it would be just another two to three months from this visit. I was beaming inside. It was the best news I could have wished for. I put the work in and now I had an idea for a return to the pitch. I would be playing again that season and I was over the moon!

"The secret is keeping busy, and loving what you do." - Lionel Hampton

Chapter 16 - Keeping Busy

As the club paid for my surgery, I had a sense of guilt due to the high cost of my injury which isn't fully covered by the GAA insurance scheme. I felt as if I owed the club the money as they were going to be out of pocket. I began to get more involved in the club and offered to help out in any fundraising. I came up with a fundraising idea that raised a thousand euro but still felt I could do more. I organised a club auction where we gathered items anyone wanted to get rid of or donate. Again, I made another thousand euro for the club that day. I was starting to enjoy the feeling of getting involved with the club off the field and they really appreciated the help. The AGM came around and my name was thrown out there for club public relations officer or PRO as it is called, which I accepted. It gave me a lift to think they trusted me with this position. I felt good to be a part of something and it would also keep me busy while I was getting back to full fitness.

This new role meant writing home match reports for games and emailing them to the local newspaper. I would also update social media sites and send notices of any events or games to the local church newsletter. I was becoming more known in and around my new club. I got roped into helping out with the next fundraiser and took on the role as secretary of the big annual fundraiser. I was looking forward to the buzz of it. I have to say it was hectic but it gave me an outlet and I didn't have time to think. I really enjoyed it and when the work I had done was evident on the night of the fundraiser it was all worthwhile. I got to sit at the top table which meant sitting next to ex-Meath footballer and RTE pundit, Colm O'Rourke and the legend that is Jimmy Magee. I remember staying over that night in the hotel and the next morning I rang our chairman to come down to join me for breakfast. While I waited for him I asked the lady at the breakfast check in, if she could check if Jimmy Magee had been down for breakfast yet. She told me that he hadn't, so I asked if she would ring his room. She did and passed the phone to me where I invited him down to join us for breakfast. We sat for nearly two hours that morning listening to stories about Mohammad Ali. He talked about all the different Olympics and World Cups he was at and names like Carl Lewis, Barry McGuigan, Michael Johnson, Pele, Maradona were being mentioned and I was in awe. He saw all the greats and he was reminiscing like it was yesterday. It was amazing and such a huge honour to be sitting beside this Irish commentary legend. This was one of the perks of working behind the scenes at the club. It was also helping me build my confidence as my efforts were really appreciated, so it gave me an enormous boost. Local people liked to see young lads helping out and I was glad to be able to do it. Later that year I received an invite to go to an inaugural county sports awards ceremony where I was so honoured to receive an award for PRO of the Year! I was so surprised. I never expected an award for a job I was happy to do. Even to be asked to an award ceremony honouring the best sports stars in the county was amazing. I was very humbled.

"There are far better things ahead than any we leave behind." - C.S. Lewis

Chapter 17 - New Season - New Me

A new football season started and the manager from two years ago decided to come back. He was there for my first season and he was appointed back in as our manager after the year off. It was great to see him back alongside our old manager who had great experience….two men I respected and they respected me. As an injured player it was hard to watch your teammates training and training so hard in preseason. I knew I should be in there with them and hurting alongside them. The good thing was that I lost loads of weight as I was so focussed at getting back to full fitness. I hoped I would take less time to get fit now with this extra weight gone. My weight had dropped for other reasons already explained in Chapter One but I wasn't showing this when I was out and about. I got a boost in energy when I would drag myself out of the house and get to the pitch. As the weeks went on I was now at the stage where I could get my boots on and join my teammates on the pitch for the lighter training. Progress was slow but it was progress. I knew I couldn't do everything they were doing but I did what I could and also followed my own training plan.

Each week my exercises became sharper and quicker. I was building more and more movement and incorporating more turning and zig zag movements at a slow pace. One evening the training schedule allowed me to start running. It felt good and I was pushing it. I tried to turn at a cone very slowly while running at a good pace. Suddenly I felt a nip. I had just torn my hamstring but it wasn't too serious. It was a warning to pace my recovery. This meant a delay in getting back and I was angry with myself but it could have been worse and it was a warning. It meant no running for a few weeks but I could still work on my knee and keep building strength using weights. The tear set me back a few weeks but I didn't let it get me down. I still had time. When it healed, I started to join in the training and more and more ball work and then eventually into full contact games. The season was well more than half way through at this stage and I had now missed eight league games. We weren't doing too well. I had my sights set on a particular league game to make my comeback in and I was feeling strong. My knee was feeling solid but maybe just not 100%. I knew I would be well able for at least thirty minutes. My target game day arrived and I was togging out. It felt so good to be putting back on a jersey with the hope of getting some game time. It was against my old friend from the physio's waiting room. The guy who told me I was finished. We were playing his team and this was my secret return date. I met him as we walked out for the warm up. He was shocked to see me in my training gear and he asked how my recovery was going and if I was anywhere close to getting back to playing. I told him I was getting there but I wouldn't tell him I was going to be playing that day, all going well. He told me that I was mad to be there and should take another few months to get myself right as I was too old. He said it took him twelve months and reminded me again that was when he was in his twenties, not 34 or 35 like I was. I made excuses for him, like that the operations had come a long way since then but in my head I was just saying that I was hungrier and wanted it more.

The game started and as expected I was on the bench. I hoped to get a few minutes at the end to test out my knee but with just ten minutes gone, our full back pulled his hamstring. He waved to the bench.... he was gone. "Niall warm up" was the call. "Yeee ha"...The buzz I got was unreal. I took off my training top, stuck the gum shield in and on I went. I jogged by my old buddy and gave him a wink. His mouth was open and eyes were shocked like he had seen a ghost. Point proved! I AM BACK!!!

Everyone who I spoke to who had cruciate operations always told me that afterwards you're not the same player you were. That fear may set in. They said you may be afraid of a tackle or that you will be very wary of your knee when landing on it. There was only one way to find out.

The ball was kicked to space and was there to be won. I was fresh on the pitch and decided to make a late run for this free ball but I knew it was not my ball to win. This didn't seem to concern me as I wanted to get stuck in so I went at full speed.... BAM!!!!! I cleaned the midfielder out coming in with my left leg very late. My timing was awful and it was a clear free. After that crashing tackle, I thought that was one way to get the nerves out of the way. I definitely felt that one, but it was just good to be back on the field. I had just given myself a serious dead left leg but I didn't care. I jogged back into position and played the rest of the game. I survived the game with no problems apart from a serious dead leg.

With game one out of the way and no problems with my knee, the next two games were coming quick and fast with a midweek and weekend game ahead. I needed to get my dead leg sorted. It was black and purple from my ankle to my hip. I did a right good job on it. I asked our chairman/physio to give it a rub and holy mackerel did he do just that. My leg was purple as bruising is caused from burst blood vessels under the skin. He said he had to break up the blood to get the stiffness out of it. I thought he was trying to kill me when he started on my leg. If I had a stick handy I would have bitten down on it and I would have probably snapped it. He had softened it up but I was still in some pain. I togged out for the midweek away game but I could still barely move my leg. My leg was now dark purple and it looked wicked. It looked broken and the lads thought it was hilarious to do that in my first game back after my long injury lay off. I was still hungry to play this game and the manager reluctantly gave me ten minutes at the end for a run out to stretch my legs. Deep down I knew I needed to rest but was I trying to do all I could to get some time on the pitch not to mention help the team if I could. I also had a point to prove that I could play. I wanted to show that I had no after-effects of the operation and also show I did not have any fear.

The weekend game came which was a home game and the scene of my cruciate injury the previous July. I hadn't played a game here since then. The game started and I was on the bench again. The bruising had settled and was now a mix of yellow and green and not as angry looking. I was called to warm up with about twenty minutes of the game to go. I ran on with a cheer from the crowd. It was great to be back on my home field and the fear was definitely gone after a few minutes when I got the first ball. Championship was approaching again and I was so eager as I had missed out on last year's championship. These are the games you train for all year and what football is all about. That weekend the junior championship draw had been made. The format changed and it was now a group round robin with three teams in a group. We got a horrible draw and we were drawn with two of the toughest teams. They were the two favourites but to win it meant beating anyone we met along the way. My fitness was getting better and the knee was holding up for longer in the games. My knee was in a bit of pain after the games and training sessions but after a few days it would be fine again. Rest and some ice helped recovery and I would be ready for the next game. I never told anyone about the pain as it was up to me to manage it. I told everyone and especially the managers that the knee was perfect and I was flying and raring to go.

Championship day wasn't long coming around. I thought I had done enough to start but was unsure as we had good competition for positions now. The team was called out and I was named in the starting fifteen. I was delighted as my work paid off but I kept my delight to myself as by me starting it meant someone else had missed out. I was named as a wing back to mark one of the opposition's best players. He was quick and after a few minutes I knew how he played. He looked for the early ball out in front and he was their target man. I knew I had to stay tight and I often stood in front of him and played from the front. As the game went on I won ball after ball whether I had to dive and get a punch on it or get out in front and win it cleanly. They moved my man into the full forward line which is a good sign for me, as he was getting nothing with me on him. A second player arrived for me to mark but he got nothing either and he was soon subbed off. The third man was struggling to get his hands on the ball and I kept him quiet for the end of the game. I was holding my own but we were trailing the whole game. We struggled in other areas of the pitch and we couldn't get a break. The final whistle blew and we lost by seven points. I gave it everything that day but it wasn't enough to get over the line. We were gutted as we had such hope... but it wasn't over. We had another shot at it and needed to win the second game or we were out.

The local newspaper had started publishing a team of the week. They were picking fifteen players from all levels who played each weekend in the championship. Fifteen players from the senior, intermediate and junior championships would make this team of the week. That Wednesday evening the newspaper came out and my name appeared at left half back. I had made the team of the week for the whole county. I was so chuffed. People had said I played well and I knew I kept my man scoreless and made some good runs. The hard work all year paid off. When I saw my name I was delighted and I thought of all my old managers who wrote me off without even seeing me play. I know they saw my name that week so it was two fingers to them... but more importantly I was vindicated.

We now had two weeks to get ourselves right as the pressure was on now for the next game. The fixtures were set and we were picked to play in our county headquarters 'Breffni Park' in a double header. We were the first game and following us was the main event where my old team would be playing straight after us. This meant my old team's supporters would be watching as most would usually come early to watch both games. As soon as I saw the double header my nerves kicked in. I felt immediate pressure that all eyes would be on me and I didn't like this. Deep down I always had a point to prove and this was on the county pitch with a big crowd on championship day. I tried to forget about it and told myself to just try your best and forget about the crowd. Match day came and I held on to my starting position at wing half back. The game started but I wasn't myself and I just couldn't tune into the game. I was looking at the crowd and nervous knowing my old team was watching and judging me. We lost one of our best forwards to a black card after only two minutes but we battled to the end and lost by a mere point. I held my hands up, I wasn't focussed that day. I would not make team of the week this week and that was a guarantee. The season was over yet again and time for an early bath. We were all gutted after all the hard work put in again this year. I was proud of getting back to playing so quickly and making the starting championship team after my recovery but another year without silverware meant there was nothing really to be proud of. So much for the third time lucky. It was back to the drawing board again and time to see where it all went wrong.

"The magic thing about home is that it feels good to leave, and it feels even better to come back." - Wendy Wunder

Chapter 18 – Home

Huge changes in my personal life meant I was moving back to my own parish. I also lost one of my best friends to cancer so I had lots of trauma to deal with. I needed people more than ever now. I wondered if my old club would want me back after leaving them three years before. I knew my transfer away didn't go down well with some people in the community. I still had passion and desire to play and I knew I could offer something for the second team. Luckily for me the two joint managers welcomed me back with open arms and I joined in a team preseason training and bonding weekend to Donegal. There were so many new young lads on the team I didn't know but it was like I never left. When I started playing reserve football back in the day, it was invaluable to have a few of the older players on the team with experience and to look after the younger players. Training was tougher than I remember but then my body wasn't getting any younger but I got stuck in as always. My body was showing signs like a retired boxer making a comeback but in my case this wasn't for a big payday. I had lots of miles in the legs and I just wasn't as sharp or as quick as I once was but I still had the experience of the old fighter. I really enjoyed putting my club jersey back on. It felt like closure that I got a chance to put it back on and play again while also getting to know the future senior players of the club. I was really enjoying my football again and my fitness was good.

We played a few challenge matches and I was getting into shape and enjoying football. We had two great managers who were both so positive. They gave me a role to play in the fullback line and I was grateful for their trust. Our first league game of the season was a home game and we were playing a strong team who were loaded with senior players as their senior team was not playing this particular weekend. It was actually the same team I made my senior debut against nearly twenty years before this. The sun was shining and the conditions were perfect. I felt good and was proud to be playing for my club again. It was nip and tuck and after about fifteen minutes I was playing the ball out of the backs. I played a one two and gave a hand pass and ran on for the return side stepping a tackle. Out of nowhere I got a full blown shoulder from the front into the ribs. I never saw it coming so I didn't have time to brace myself so I was not prepared. It was like a car crash you might see at an intersection. I was like the driver driving through on a green light singing away to himself and the other player was a crazy driver breaking the red light and just ploughed straight through me. So out of nowhere I took a hit, down I went in serious pain. I found it hard to breathe as I hadn't taken a breath or seen him coming. I heard a few cracks on impact so I definitely cracked or broke a rib or two. I gasped for air and opened my eyes with a grimace. It felt like all the air was taken out of my lungs at once. I wasn't one to stay down on the ground even when I was hurt so I got to my feet sharpish. I wouldn't like to let the other player know he hurt me no matter what injury I had. I got to my feet and the magic water bottle was there held by my manager. I took a swig and looked at the ref with my teacher's look and said to her "what was that?".

She reached for her pocket and out came a yellow. She waved it at number ten. Unbelievable! I nodded my head in disbelief, said nothing.

It was a blatant reckless tackle to take me out that clearly deserved a red card. I never saw a referee change their mind... so no point arguing. I held my ribs, took a deep breath and jogged back to my position. Every breath and step I took hurt and it was still only the first half. When a referee gives a yellow card for a tackle like that you can judge what is acceptable to this referee. So now I knew where the bar was and it was going to be that kind of a game. I had revenge on my mind and I had plenty of time left in the game. A few minutes later I spotted 'my old friend' number ten on a solo run. This guy was 6 foot 2 inches and built like a tank but my radar was locked on him. He was bombing it up the pitch and nobody could stop him. He took five or six solos right up the middle of the pitch and he cut through players with ease. He was heading for goal, so like a heat seeking missile I made my way towards him. He was now about thirty five yards out so it was time to intercept. I planned my run and ran diagonally towards him, building up speed. I hit him with an almighty shoulder and I heard a crunch! I spun around and saw him hop the ball and it didn't knock a stride out of him. He continued on while I bounced off him like a swatted fly. He kicked the ball and it skimmed the post and wide. Then the pain hit me. My neck and shoulder seized up. I couldn't move them. I knew I had done some serious damage. I couldn't show he hurt me so I jogged on and took up my position just hoping the ball would not be kicked anywhere near me. I looked at the clock and it was close to half time. I thought to myself that I could make it until then. Minutes felt like hours and finally the half time whistle came. Thank the Lord! I struggled towards the dugout, sat down, barely able to speak as my ribs were bad, neck seized and my shoulder couldn't move. I signalled to my manager with my working arm that I was out using a side swipe movement. I couldn't even talk, never mind move both arms. I watched the second half in pain. I should have gone straight to the hospital. When the game was over I couldn't lift my arm to get my jersey off me. I remember putting out an APB on the team WhatsApp group for some pain relief like anti-inflammatories. Shortly afterwards, my doorbell rang and I got a delivery that evening of some anti-inflammatory gel. Thank you Sean! It settled me a little but I never slept that night. I was queuing at the local pharmacy the next morning before they opened looking for some pain relief. As I sat waiting, I felt like Danny Glover's character in Lethal Weapon saying to myself "I'm getting too old for this sh*t Riggs".

To this day I think back to the guy I hit with a shoulder. Maybe he was a cyborg from Terminator back looking in Virginia for John Connors and he decided to try Gaelic football that day. It was honestly like hitting metal. But then I did shoulder him with my left side which, for one, was my weaker side but also was the side I had just cracked my ribs earlier in the game. I played around with why I got hurt, making excuses that it was ribs or I hit him the wrong way. I knew I could give a good shoulder and I was known for it. The honest answer was he was twenty and ripped, I was nearly 40 and not ripped. These new breeds live in the gym and have six packs. My six pack was in the fridge! Little did I know, that was the last day I played for my beloved club.

"My heart can take the pounding, my mind can handle the grind, but my body knows it's time to say goodbye." - Kobe Bryant

Chapter 19 - Life Without Football

Life without football can be lonely. When each season ended, you welcomed the winter break to rest and recover. My season was over without warning. When you spend three days a week at the football pitch, meeting your friends, who you see more than most people, it is very hard to suddenly stop. I sat at home and the realisation hit me hard and I really missed it. The thoughts of never togging out again really hurt. I didn't think anything could match playing and I had no thoughts or interest in management. I didn't believe I would be any good. A close friend of mine called me up one day and asked if I would come back to help as a selector with the reserve team for the following year. I reluctantly told him that I would but I had my doubts if I would enjoy it. When I went to the games it instantly felt like I was back part of a team again. Some of my friends were still playing alongside some of the younger lads. I was given my club polo shirt with my initials on it and I was grateful to be now helping out. It filled the void of not playing. Every year there were some new faces who were going to be the next stars. The following year I was asked to help with the Under-17 team. My first thought was to say no, but no doesn't work. I was convinced to come in and I got to know some of the future talent. That year we won the league and the following year we won a local tournament so it was a successful few years.

In 2016 our senior team were in great form and after twenty four years we won the senior county championship. What a day! It was a dream of mine to be on a winning senior championship team but it was not to be, but it didn't dampen the celebrations. I always felt that all past players and managers had a part to play in this victory. When I played we survived so many relegation battles to keep the club at senior level. All the previous managers also were building the team and we finally did it. We had so many hard-fought games for the club over the years… so it was not just about the twenty-five squad players, it was a win for every past player that had worn the black and amber.

One year we entered an intermediate team so it meant we had three men's teams. I was honoured to be asked if I would co-manage our club's men's reserve team, which would be the junior team. We were managing the Killer B's! The team I started to play for back over twenty years ago. It was an honour to be asked. We had a great team and we were going well in the championship but the season was abruptly cut short with a Covid lockdown. We never finished the season but I just loved being involved. It is amazing how things go full circle from playing to managing and it is just amazing to be involved in my club. It was such a great way to get to know the new players coming through. Some of these players on this team and on the Under-17 team went on to win the Championship in 2021 when we lifted the cup again. I was club PRO at this stage so I was involved in reporting on all games sometimes in empty stadiums during Covid. I was close to the action, and being back on the sidelines with the squad felt great.

An old team mate asked me in as a selector for our ladies senior team. I initially said 'No' but I was talked into it and the plan was to win the championship after a few barren years. That first year we made the county final but unfortunately we were beaten on the day. I have to admit it was a hugely enjoyable year with some seriously talented players. I knew there was something special about this squad and the following year they won the Championship. I was a very quiet part of the management in the second year but the girls loved seeing me coming to the games and I felt wanted. They were an amazing bunch of girls and all so appreciative of all the time we gave up to be there.

Getting involved in management after playing was one of the best things I did. It brought me back into the club and I felt that I was a part of the club again. It is not the same as playing but it is the next best thing. Every club in the country is run by volunteers giving up their time to make the club run. It is not easy but if you have a love for the game, it makes it easy.

"Hard work will always overcome natural talent when natural talent does not work hard enough."
- Alex Ferguson

Chapter 20 - One Life - One Club?

Without a doubt football has helped me get over some very dark days. Coming together with a bunch of lads and playing a team sport was a lifeline for me. Lifelong friendships are formed with players of all ages. It's not all about winning, although that is a special feeling. It is all about meeting up at training and games, having a chat and letting off some steam. Everyone needs some exercise to help reduce stress and relax so what better place to do than with your friends. If I was asked for one piece of advice I would say - enjoy it, believe in yourself and don't listen to anyone but yourself. I have had some inspirational managers along with some terrible managers at both school and club level. The terrible ones should have made me quit but I loved the game too much and I didn't value their ignorant comments. The damage some people who are in all types of management positions and in power can inflict on good people without knowing it, or maybe some do and they just don't care, can have such detrimental effects on people's confidence for a lifetime. When criticism or rejection happens over and over again it chips away at a person's self esteem until they feel worthless and give up. This damage makes them feel so unworthy of anything good. Exclusion is a form of bullying. The feeling of not being good enough will affect your life in so many ways. But you are better than that, so do not quit. Show these bullies in any way that you can that they made a huge mistake. Prove them wrong. Don't give up doing something you love for these clobs! If you are reading this and struggling secretly inside, please reach out and talk to someone. Pick a friend you know who will listen to you. Make sure to pick someone who will listen and support you.

Listening is huge, as some people will listen for a minute but then tell you all about their lives for thirty minutes. Some may give you a lecture on what you should or shouldn't do! So be careful who you choose but you won't be long finding out who these people are. It may take a few goes to get the right person. You may even meet a new friend who knows what it is like to feel like you do. If you can, choose a positive person who understands and really cares. Avoid the drainer who wants to suck your remaining energy so they can feel a little better about themselves. Again you won't be long finding out who the drainers are as you will be shattered when you leave their company, so start limiting your time with these people, and increasing your time with the people who make you feel good about yourself when you leave. When you meet these kinds of people you feel so energised and so much more positive. People like this are there to lift you and they want you to do well. They will welcome a text if you are not feeling great. By even sending a message like this it will be a big step into opening up and telling them you may be struggling. I promise you that they will be so glad you reached out to them and they will be honoured to help you, their friend. If this is too hard just text or call a freephone helpline. They are there to listen and not judge. Remember these people are kind and caring and will do their best to help you. It may be just one call or one text but you will be so proud of yourself having the courage to do it. There should be no stigma anymore for anyone who needs a little help or counselling. I always remember what my GP said "One in three people have some form of depression", so it is only when you talk about it you realise so many people are in the same boat. You may even help each other.

Listening is so important for people who are suffering. Recently I was out for a walk on the beach late one evening when the tide was out. I noticed a person sitting on some rocks which were usually submerged. I had my headphones in but I could hear a shout and realised that this guy was calling me. My first thoughts were that he might be looking for money or a cigarette but as I thought about it more, why would he be on a beach if he wanted money? I stopped in my tracks and looked over and could see this guy really wanting me to come over. I reluctantly walked over, unsure of what to expect. As I got closer, I could see it was a man in his early thirties sitting there crying. He was grey in the face and very underweight. He was so thankful I stopped as he just wanted to talk to someone. He sat there hoping someone would walk by. He told me he was in a vicious circle of drinking and drugs and that he was sick of it all but couldn't stop. He told me a search party was out looking for him and he was expecting the lifeguard to arrive. He hated himself and wanted it all to end. He told me that he used to play football with the local club, had a little girl but when his relationship ended he turned to drink and drugs. He sat crying on the rocks, drinking out of a bottle of wine and told me he was contemplating walking into the sea and finishing it all. I listened and reassured him that life would get better. I reminded him of his little daughter who would have no father if he did anything and she would be devastated. This seemed to hit him and he asked if he could walk with me. We strolled along the beach and chatted away and thankfully he agreed to walk to the local Garda station with me. When we got to the gates, he made excuses and wanted to go get his wallet to buy more wine first but I convinced him to just pop into the station first. There I explained to the Garda on the desk and she said she would look after him. He was now in a safe place. He shook my hand and told me I had just saved his life. I was just so glad I turned around on the beach and I listened to this man in desperate need.

If you are a manager of a team or a manager of staff in a company reading this, be kind and think of the damage you do by your words. If you leave the same players on the bench every week you are destroying their confidence and they will eventually quit. Please give every player a chance, praise them, encourage them and build their confidence. Catch the player doing well, afford freedom, encourage imagination, reward effort and be kind. Poor managers cost clubs so many players every year. Is it any wonder why you could have around sixty or eighty under sixes at training and then twelve years later you might be doing well to have just one or two coming through to play senior football? Managers of underage teams should strive for effort, not results. Strive for inclusion and progression. Strive for retention and not trophies. The best players now may not be the best players in the future. The weakest players now may be the best players in the future. Children develop at different times so give them a chance. Poor managers at underage levels are destroying the potential of clubs. Equally if you manage people in a company, be kind and treat staff with respect. Give Respect. Get Respect! Don't abuse your power to bully. Good leaders will show how things are done and lead staff, not wait til they make a mistake and attack them. "When it's club, It lives forever" is a new ad campaign for the GAA. Managers need to remember that criticism and bullying live forever too!

For the person who is struggling, self care is so important. This will be hard but try to put the phone away. We all get hypnotised by them and spend hours scrolling through so much rubbish on social media which will not have enhanced our lives one bit. Do we feel better after? We all know the answer is no. Looking at these people with huge houses, amazing cars and perfect bodies only makes us all feel less inadequate than when we started. When our mood is low we need to listen or read some positive pieces from people who have come out the other side of low moods or depression. Try to listen to a podcast or a meditation instead. When we listen to people who have come out of a dark place they have some great advice to get yourself back on track. I found Pat Divilly, a Galway man, very easy to listen to and I could relate to so many of his stories. There are so many great "life coaches" like Pat out there, so just find one you can listen to and relate to.

I am so grateful to my friends who phoned me every week when I was very low. As bad as things can feel at the time, it is amazing how quickly your mood can turn and change back to being more positive. It works the other way too, where out of the blue you go from laughing to being very low. There are triggers all around and sometimes we don't know what made our mood change so drastically and so quickly. Please give yourself time to rest, sleep in and give yourself some time to let some light in again. Dark days may return but try to remember that your mood can change quickly again. Don't beat yourself up when you drop. Remember people care for you. More people care for you than you think. In Japan, broken pottery is often repaired with gold. The flaw is seen as a unique piece of the object's history, which adds to its beauty. We all have cracks and the key is that when we repair them we learn from them and become a better and more beautiful person by understanding more about ourselves. We all have our flaws and when we accept that nobody on this earth is perfect we can learn to live a happier life.

I am so grateful to the current club chairman who phoned me when I was very low. He asked me to come back to help out with my home club as an underage selector. Even though I said no, he persisted and convinced me to help out. This was the best thing I did and without a doubt it helped my confidence, not to mention getting to know so many new players. I am deeply grateful for him not giving up on me and pushing me as it got me out of my house in the evenings. I am also thankful to a former club chairman for asking me to be the club PRO and later the joint manager of the reserve team. I am so thankful for my friend asking me in as a selector and my other friend for asking me to help with the ladies team. All these things brought me back involved in the club and community that I had missed so much. I never thought I would be involved in management but it was a life saver. I was never great with the actual coaching but I praised every player and gave them confidence if they made a mistake. If I saw a player struggling I would encourage them. This was my strength as a selector as I was a player who played better when my confidence was high, so I knew what feeling good meant. I played so much better with managers who believed in me. I feel I brought a good energy around the team and I think all players saw this. Being in management is not the same as playing but it is as close as you can get when you physically can't play anymore. Every club needs people to help and your club will be so glad to have you there in any capacity. There are always jobs to be done. Without these people behind the scenes, there would be no GAA clubs.

The motto 'One Life - One Club' never sat right with me. Some of the biggest advocates for this motto have spent summers in America and transferred to American clubs and made a few bob for their services. Does this not count? If your home GAA club does not play hurling or rounders, you are allowed to play for other clubs that play these sports. So in fact you are entitled to play for three different clubs at the one time - football, hurling and rounders should you wish. I joined a rounders club in Dublin recently and in my first year we won a Dublin League and made it as far as an All-Ireland Semi Final. Each base is just 25m apart so I knew I could manage these short run without seizing up. So, if I look back I have in fact played for four clubs. In my opinion that motto is outdated and for narrow-minded people. To me, it's all about playing and doing something you love. It would have been much easier for me to hang up my boots when I was sitting on the bench for all those years but I made a tough choice. As I always think to myself "You are the artist of your own life. Do not give the paintbrush to anyone else". I chose to continue playing football and I am glad I did because this was the game I loved. I don't hold any grudges against anyone. In fact I am so thankful to my home club for allowing me to transfer and continue to play football. It was each manager's personal opinion that stopped me getting any football so I do not blame the club at all. Both local clubs are such wonderful clubs with passionate supporters and hard working committees. I feel honoured to have played with both and I have great memories. I am so grateful my home club took me back again after my few years away. Have I any regrets? None. Does anyone else's opinion on my transfer matter to me? No!

"What is the bravest thing you've ever said? asked the boy. 'Help,' said the horse. 'Asking for help isn't giving up,' said the horse. 'It's refusing to give up." -Charlie Mackesy, The Boy, the Mole, the Fox and the Horse

Chapter 21- Tips for People to Help Understand

When someone has opened up to you about his/her anxiety or depression, just sit and listen. All I wanted was someone to listen when I was actually able to speak. Some days I couldn't even physically open my mouth and sometimes when I did, no words would come out. To have someone sitting with me meant the world. It was a glimmer that someone cared and understood the pain a little. Somedays I could talk and try to explain the pain and thoughts I was having, other days nothing.... but to have someone who texts, phones or pops by to see you and just sit in silence helps. There are days the curtains will stay closed and I will be hiding from everyone but please don't give up calling. These are the days I needed company the most but just too low to get out of bed to open the door. Don't take this personally. Please keep calling. Ideally get a key and come in and make two cups of coffee, drop one in and sit on the end of the bed and tell them you are there for them. This would have given me such a boost. One thing you will need is patience. There will be days of pure silence and not a word spoken and maybe no response to your questions. Please be patient. Sometimes my mouth couldn't get the words out to explain. Please do not shout and slam the door in frustration when you are not getting a response. This really makes things so much worse as then we feel even more pain and suffering as we frustrate you. It is so hard but when people showed me their annoyance it set me back so much and I used to say what's the point looking for help when nobody understands. We then pull the blankets over our faces and sink deeper into the depression. Please, please have patience as we do come out of this dark hole eventually. Bear with us and just sit there and reassure us that things will be ok and that you care for us. Please do offer tea, food and if no reply comes, please just drop up a cup and some food. If it's not eaten, don't worry but sometimes a bite will be taken and a sip will be drunk and this is progress. Keep showing love and patience and hold back on any negatives. It is like someone in hospital breaking a leg. Don't expect them to be able to walk the next day. Give them time to heal and just encourage and show love and once they know you are there this helps.

The worst thing anyone can do is try to tell someone what to do. The amount of times I was told to get up and get out and about. Go for a walk or get back into a routine as it's good for you. You will feel better. In theory, of course I would have done but when you are so low, the thoughts of getting dressed is huge. Then the anxiety of leaving the house. Who might I meet if I go for a run or walk? What if they ask me why I am not at work? What if they ask me if I am ok? What should I say? Will I break down and cry? The monkey mind kicks in and tells me I am safer at home and just stay where you are.

If you think of someone you know who may be struggling, reach out to them. Drop them a text or make an effort to talk to them. Drive to their house with a coffee, sit with them and make them know they are important. Even if you sit with them in silence and show you care. Even to know you are there and just to listen means so much. They will try to say they are busy and put off meeting up. If you arrive at their house, they may not even let you in. They will make excuses that they are busy but please, please don't give up on them. Trust me, please just keep in contact. When they push you away and tell you that they are fine, be kind and don't lose patience with them. It is easy to say that you tried and they didn't want help but deep down they are hoping that you don't give up but they just can't say it. Maybe they are not ready to talk just yet so give them a day or two and try again. If they talk, just listen. Don't talk over and start talking about your own problems. Ask them how they feel and show them you are there for them and that your phone is on 24/7. Even telling them this will instantly make them not feel alone and that someone understands and cares.

When a person is in a deep depression they are in a haze. It is very hard for people to explain how it feels. When I was there, I couldn't even use my voice or get a word out of my mouth. I was that low that talking seemed so hard but also like a waste of time. If someone did call, even by just being there to make them tea or bring them some food meant so much. Sending a text means a lot and it shows someone is thinking of them and cares for them. Please continue to show signs that you are thinking of them. Send jokes and try to make them laugh to start with. Eventually you could try to get them to go out for a walk, join a new class or even get them to come back to playing football. If they have stopped playing, even ask would they help out with the football club in some other role as there are always jobs going as selectors or committee members. Rally together as a team and try to get them back involved in any small way. Offer to collect them to watch a game so they can feel wanted and involved. When they say 'No' arrive anyway and tell them they are coming with you.

When I went very low it was a dark and scary place to be. I had no energy, there was no light getting in at all. It was so hard to find joy in anything. If someone told me I had won the lottery, I would find it hard to crack a smile. If someone tried to help and do a nice deed for me, I may not have been able to show gratitude. If you try to help someone in a similar situation and don't get the response you expected, please don't react badly. If for example you spend hours cleaning their house, they may not actually care as the state of the house will be the least of their worries. You may feel better for trying to help but we can not see past the pain. You may end up feeling so annoyed or your efforts under appreciated but we are not able to see any good in anything. Deep down it is appreciated but nothing means much at that time. The only thing we want to feel is to feel better.

Usually you don't want to see anyone and you start getting images of what it might be like if you were not around anymore. It is like you are in so much pain inside that your body is screaming at you to just end it. You often hear the analogy of dark clouds but it feels like a dark force pushing your shoulders down and smothering you slowly. All your positivity and spark is sucked out of your body and you feel like you're drowning in mud. Your voice is gone, your body is tired but your mind never stops racing. Every negative situation plays on repeat in your mind. You get more paranoid about people and make every good memory seem the opposite.

I could never hurt anyone so why would I hurt people who love me and disappear where they would never find answers. It would be such punishment for everyone. I had to find a way out of this blackness. I had to get out of this and be kind to myself in the process. Little by little I would get myself up and even drive to a different town to get a coffee or some shopping. I generally did this so I would avoid people I knew. I felt unknown in other towns so I could get a coffee and walk around with more confidence. Somedays I would drive to a scenic spot and drink my coffee taking in the scenery around me. These little things gave me a lift. I loved taking pictures and I was told I had a keen eye for spotting a nice picture. I didn't have a camera but my phone was decent so I took photos of sunsets, nature, clouds and I sent them to my local paper. They always made it to print so these little things gave me a boost that I was good at something. The hoped-for "Likes" on Facebook can give people with depression such a boost so be kind when someone posts a picture. It's amazing when you get a few nice comments and "Likes"... it does actually lift your spirits. The key is to get through the darkest days and the light will shine slowly at first but it always gets brighter. I am becoming better at catching myself getting low and trying to do something before I get dangerously low but it can creep up on you out of nowhere. Some days I am laughing and joking and then that same night I go quiet and start to sink. Awareness is huge. When I see this happening now, I go get some air or some space and sit with it and see what's happening. I think 'what just happened that made me drop my mood?'. Try to find what exactly happened so you know what triggered you. I generally try to meditate or listen to tranquil music so it's nice and peaceful. Sometimes for an hour or two, whatever is needed to bring me back. I have found a few great podcasts like, as I mentioned earlier, Pat Divilly or even read some books. I found reading so difficult as my mind was going a million miles an hour. To focus on words was too hard. I found I had to calm my mind first, then try to read a little at a time. The key is to put the distractions like the phone away, get a quiet spot and open page one and see how you go. If you read half a page, it is progress. It is getting into a routine and giving yourself this time as much as possible. It is a slow process but it is progress and one step up a ladder at a time is progress.

Sometimes when I think back to those dark moments I try to make sense of why I would want to leave this world but you are not in your right mind. You are not thinking straight. It is almost like you are possessed by a dark force who wants you to give up. You honestly cannot see any light and there is no glimmer. Only for the mental strength I had I fought hard and always got a positive image in my head. It wasn't easy but I had so much to live for. So many people who loved me and I knew I had so much potential and I was too young to leave. Never give up. There is always hope! As bad as the feelings you have at the time and when you are at the lowest you have felt, please know things will always get better. There may seem to be no way out but there always is. If you thought of all the people who think how amazing you are, not to mention all the people in the world you haven't yet met. Life can seem hopeless but there is so much we haven't done. If your job is getting to you and you feel stuck, start to think of your perfect day. What would you do if you could do it everyday? Now, how can I do this? How much money will I need to survive? Do I need certain things or are they luxuries I can survive without? Maybe it's the people you hang around with. Ask yourself, are these people making me feel better or worse after I spend time with them? You know what to do, if you feel worse after spending time with them. You need to find genuine friends who will help you feel better and not be there to make their lives feel better. If it is money problems, write down all your outgoings and incomings and work on a plan. What if you cut back on some expenses, would you survive?

There is always hope for a new start and it is never too late to start. Life is for living and enjoying, not working in a job you hate until you are too old to enjoy your retirement properly. Do something you enjoy and wake up in the morning saying that you love your job. It is not always that simple with mortgages and outgoings but try to do something you love each day. I was listening to one of Pat Divilly's podcasts recently and he talked about how we should mirror the seasons of nature. There is a time for planting seeds, a time for looking after the crops, a time for harvesting and a time for hibernation. There can be a lot of pressure in society to be constantly producing. This is not how nature works. Similar to ourselves, there needs to be a time for rest and hibernation where we go into the dark to rest, prepare and learn. We can then emerge, revitalised with new opportunity and plant new seeds and be ready to go again. We need to be kind to ourselves and nurture ourselves.

We can learn a lot from Winnie The Pooh and Piglet's friendship when Piglet knew Winnie was having a bad day. Winnie didn't want to talk about it but Piglet didn't walk away as he knew it was important to be there for his friend.

"Today was a Difficult Day," said Pooh.
There was a pause.
"Do you want to talk about it?" asked Piglet.
"No," said Pooh after a bit. "No, I don't think I do."
"That's okay," said Piglet, and he came and sat beside his friend.
"What are you doing?" asked Pooh.
"Nothing, really," said Piglet. "Only, I know what Difficult Days are like. I quite often don't feel like talking about it on my Difficult Days either."
"But goodness," continued Piglet, "Difficult Days are so much easier when you know you've got someone there for you. And I'll always be here for you, Pooh."
And as Pooh sat there, working through in his head his Difficult Day, while the solid, reliable Piglet sat next to

him quietly, swinging his little legs...he thought that his best friend had never been more right.

A.A. Milne

"On your darkest days do not try to see the end of the tunnel by looking far ahead. Focus only on where you are right now. Then carefully take one step at a time, by placing just one foot in front of the other. Before you know it, you will turn that corner." - Anthon St. Maarten

Chapter 22 - Nice Things to do for Yourself

Retreats

Book yourself into a one day or weekend retreat. There are so many retreats available now to help with anxiety, depression or just over-coming some fears. Again, Pat Divilly, amongst many more people, offers these retreats or evening talks. You will find that everyone who goes to these events are all like minded people so the atmosphere is always amazing, where so many brave people have made this huge step in getting themselves back on track. There are even lovely retreats around Ireland where you can book and stay and engage in daily meditations and a quiet place to read and just unwind. I went to an amazing place at the start of my re-discovery in Cork. A few days to read, get away from social media and just switch off. It was such an amazing few days where I got to spend time on myself and write this book in pure bliss whilst watching the crystal blue waves of the Atlantic Ocean below me. There is also a very deep amazing weekend called The ManKind Project for men who want to go back to their inner child and do some deep work. An amazing weekend.... but it is not for everyone. I was prepared to try anything and I was so glad I did.

Spiritual Healers

Some people may be wary but there are so many amazingly gifted people out there who will help you overcome your anxiety and fears. I have to say my new partner, Aoife, has helped me so much. She not only helped me overcome so much trauma but guided me to so many other gifted people around the world who could help me be stronger and give me so many techniques to use to protect myself from energy vampires or to recover quicker. Spiritual healing may not be everyone's cup of tea but when I was so low, I tried anything and I really can say, it is amazing. So to my spiritual healers in America, England, Scotland, Australia and Ireland I thank you so much.

Sleep on, rest and do not feel guilty

Never feel guilty if you need to have a lie on some mornings or every morning. This is your body telling you, you need it. Alternatively, if you feel you perform better getting up at 6am and getting out for an early morning walk before the birds get up, do this. You know what works for you. I tend to go between both and try to listen to my body. I loved a 6am start and getting out before anyone else was up. There is something very satisfying about being up and outside as the sun rises and it is just you and nature. Before most people stir in their beds, you have already conquered a walk or a run. It really is a powerful start to any day.

Meditation/Breathing

Practise some relaxation techniques like meditation, yoga or deep breathing. Meditation is easier than you may think as all you need is a nice audio clip to play on your phone, lie down and just listen. You can even snooze whilst listening as you subconsciously take it all in. There are so many lovely guided meditations on

YouTube or Spotify. Just find the one you like and save it to your phone.

I recently discovered some very powerful breathing techniques that are just amazing. Some techniques to look at are Box Breathing, Wim Hof Method and Buteyko Breathing. All different forms of controlled breathing but very powerful. When you breathe short, shallow and fast your heart rate increases. If you feel fear, get a fright or panic your heart rate instantly increases. When you take long breaths and expand your chest your heart rate slows down so you feel much calmer.

Before all breathing exercises you should get comfortable in a quiet place. Try to close your eyes and clear your busy mind whilst focusing on your breath. Take a big deep breath to start - in through your nose and out through your mouth.

Box breathing is where you take a four second inhale through your nose. Hold for four seconds and out through the mouth for four seconds, Then repeat and try to fill up your chest with deep inhales through the nose each time. As you get more used to this you can extend to 4-7-8 Breathing. So it's four seconds to inhale through the nose. Hold for seven and then exhale through the mouth for eight seconds making a whoosh sound.

The Wim Hof Method is from Wim Hof who is also known as the Iceman. This method is where you take a deep breath with your nose or mouth and out through the mouth and repeat this for 30 or 40 times in short, powerful bursts. After the last exhalation, inhale one final time as deeply as you can. Then let all the air out and hold at the end. Hold until you feel the urge to breathe again. When you feel the urge to breathe again, draw one big breath in filling your lungs. Feel your stomach and chest expanding. When you have the biggest breath you can take, hold this for 15 seconds then let go. That is one full round complete. This can be repeated 3 or 4 times.

There are many other breathing methods like a controlled breathing and holding of the breath called the Buteyko Method that you may also like.

Listen to an audio book or Podcast

When you are anxious, your mind races from one thing to the next and it is impossible to focus on reading. Even when you get to the point of opening a book that has been lying on your bedside locker for years, reading is a huge challenge. My mind just kept overthinking and I was reading words but not taking in the book. I also found I was so easily distracted by anything and always opening my phone again and again. I found getting audio books really was a huge help as I could walk and listen or listen in the car. I didn't have to read and I found listening much easier. There are so many terrific books out there to read. So many classics like 'Man's Search for Meaning' by Victor Frankl. This was such an inspiring book about a man who never gave up and the power of positivity in the darkest of places.

Open Up
Reach out to a few people who you think will help you. Do not be afraid to talk about how you are feeling. You will be surprised but your friend might be in a similar place and only too delighted you mentioned it. Even if they aren't, you will feel better for being able to talk about how you feel. Just to have at least one person as a person you can call, text or meet for a chat when times get tough.

Nature
Spend some time in nature - Go for a walk, a slow run, a cycle, or even a drive to your favourite spot with a take-away coffee. If you can "ground" yourself, even better. Grounding or earthing is just taking your shoes off and standing or walking on the grass, beach or in the water. It has huge healing remedies as it reconnects your body electrically with the earth.

Holidays
When you feel anxious or stressed sometimes we bury ourselves into something else to distract ourselves. This eventually catches up with you. I buried myself in my work but naturally enough I burnt out. So when you are feeling stressed take some time off to recharge and if you can get away for a few days do it. It is amazing the difference you feel waking up in a different place. Be good to yourself and plan some mini breaks away from your area. I love going to a new town and going for a coffee and people watch. When you do not know anyone, you feel so much more confident to do this as it is not something you can do in your own town.

Pamper Yourself
Go do something nice for yourself like get your haircut, facial, massage, nails done or just hit the shops or the cinema. By even getting dressed up a little or putting on some nice clothes and getting out of your tracksuit makes you instantly feel a little better. So trust me you will feel even better when you do something for yourself.

New Class
Keep and eye out for a new class or activity in your area. No matter what age you are there are things to do. GAA clubs are great, as some have Rounders teams that you don't have to be super fit for. The most you run is 25 meters and then stop or if you can hit a home run you have a 100 metre sprint and then a long rest. It is a great way to meet people and it is a bit of exercise too. There are so many social activities in towns now like men's sheds, golf, photography courses, computer courses and they are all a great way to meet new people.

Get a pet
If you feel lonely, think about getting a pet for company. Pets are great company and if you get a dog it will get you out of the house at least once a day when you bring it for walks.

Journalling
Daily journalling is such a great way to realise how great you are and all you have achieved. Write down all the things you like about yourself. Write down your

aims for the week, month, year, 3 years. Start to believe these are going to happen and focus everyday on how it feels when these all happen.

Finish the day with writing down all you achieved that day and write down three more aims for the next day. The next night mark off the aims achieved and continue. You will feel so much more focussed each morning waking up with three aims. These could simply be to make a call to a friend, go for coffee and read a few pages of a book. The sense of achievement every night before you go to bed gives you a boost that you are making progress and focussing on the gains and not looking at the gaps you have yet to achieve.

Doctor/GP
If you are feeling very low please do visit your GP for a chat. They do understand and it is so much more common than you think. Don't be afraid to just say that you are not feeling great and your mood is very low or you are anxious and need some help.

Counselling
There are so many free counselling services available now. It may take you time to make the call but you will be very glad you did it. The people who answer the phone are not there to judge but to help and are some of the most caring people. Some do it voluntarily so that shows how kind these people are, giving up their free time to help people who just need to vent or chat. Just remember it is a person who will not judge you, only listen and offer support. Some services that

may be of help are listed in the contact details below. Also, see Irish Association for Counselling and Psychotherapy at www.iacp.ie for a full list of your local therapists.

"There is a crack in everything. That's how the light gets in." - Leonard Cohen

Chapter 23 – Hope

Everyone always told me that things would get better but I was not sure if I ever believed them. I always had hoped that my life would improve but it would not just happen automatically. There is only one person who can decide when the time is right and that person is you. It took me years of pain and suffering to finally take the step to get some help. Firstly, with counselling... and as the years went on I worked with so many different people who all had individual skills. From reiki healers, kinesiologists, spiritual healers, life coaches, career coaches and other healers. I have booked holidays where I have gone just to read and unwind. This is all part of getting back to loving myself again. I have gone on day and weekend retreats, some of which have worked on "shadow" work and all trying to get back to the root of my trauma. We all carry parts of us that we repress, hide or deny which are our shadows. These are the parts of ourselves we feel are unloveable. We think we can hide these parts away but the more we push them away the more they run our lives. The key is to face these shadows and bring them out in front of us which is a very hard thing to do. Our shadows hold different types of traumas that we have repressed as a child but it continues to affect us as adults until we deal with them. As a child we are told to stop doing different things so we repress parts of ourselves that were deemed unacceptable. As adults we have to then go back to the 'inner child' and try to rectify these things. I have found it very powerful, as difficult as this can be to do. This work is emotional as it digs deep, but it is worth it.

I have taken a career break from a very stressful job which has given me more time for self-care and to begin a new career in helping people with mental health issues. I plan to work with more and more groups and people this year and show that there is a way out of the darkness. When I started to like myself again, I let more good people into my life which has made my life so much better. These people wanted to see me get back to myself and feel good again. One of these people, as I said earlier, my partner, Aoife, who built up my confidence with such love and lots of perseverance. I was the king of self-sabotage, so I could say I reaffirmed to myself that I would never be happy again. With depression there are, of course, still good and bad days. My aim is to make the bad days shorter and the good days to last longer and longer. I have accepted that this will be my life and I have to continue to keep working hard to keep myself positive. It is up to me to stop the pity-party and allow myself some happiness. I cannot thank Aoife enough for not giving up on me. We now have an amazing baby boy who has changed our lives so much. He is the happiest little man and has made me the happiest man again. He makes me live up to my nickname again! Smiley is back!

So when people say to you that things will get better, they will when YOU take the first step. Martin Luther King Junior said "Faith is taking the first step even when you don't see the whole staircase". Be patient, as you may still have a dip in form. Be kind with yourself on these days and take your time. Always look back on how far you have come and don't keep looking ahead at what you have yet to achieve. You will get there when the time is right. Most importantly - "Never Give Up"!

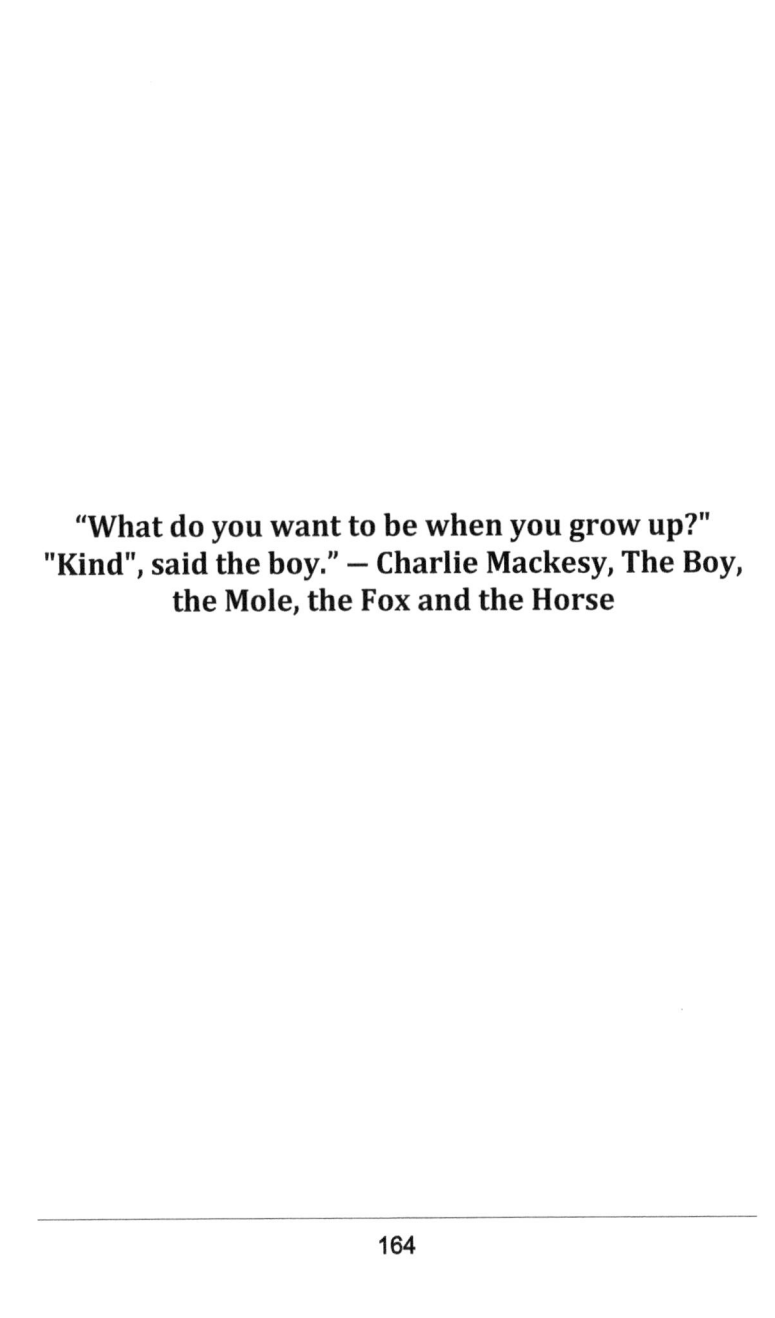

"What do you want to be when you grow up?"
"Kind", said the boy." — Charlie Mackesy, The Boy, the Mole, the Fox and the Horse

"Don't Quit"

When things go wrong, as they sometimes will,
When the road you're trudging seems all uphill,
When the funds are low but the debts are high,
And you want to smile but you have to sigh,
When care is pressing you down a bit,
Rest if you must, but don't you quit.

Life is strange with its twists and turns,
As every one of us sometimes learns,
And many failures turn about
When we might have won had we stuck it out.
Don't give up though the pace seems slow –
You may succeed with another blow.

Success is failure turned inside out –
The silver tint of the clouds of doubt,
You can never tell how close you are,
It may be near when it seems so far;
So stick to the fight when you're hardest hit –
It's when things seem worst that you must not quit.

by Edgar Albert Guest

"And once the storm is over, you won't remember how you made it through, how you managed to survive. You won't even be sure, whether the storm is really over. But one thing is certain. When you come out of the storm, you won't be the same person who walked in. That's what this storm's all about."- Haruki Murakami

- **Useful Contacts**

- Samaritans 24/7 - Phone 116 123 or samaritans.org/ireland

- Pieta House - Free 24/7 Crisis Helpline 1800247247 Text HELP to 51444

- CRISIS TEXT LINE 24/7 - Text 50808 to start the conversation

- Aware - 1800 80 4848 aware.ie

- Pieta House - 1800 247 247 - Text "HELP" to 51444 pieta.ie

- GROW - 1890 474474 - grow.ie

- Text about it - 50808 (24/7) text50808.ie

- Women's Aid - 1800 341 900 (24/7) - womensaid.ie

- Men's Aid - 01 554 3811 mensaid.ie Email: hello@mensaid.ie

- Mens Development Network - 1800 816 588 - mensnetwork.ie

- La Dolce Vita Project (NI & NW) -04871-377272 la-dolce-vita-project.com

- ALONE (Older people) 0818 222 024 or alone.ie

- Childline (Children) 1800 66 6666 - Free text: 50101 - childline.ie

- Jigsaw (Youth) 1800 544729 'Text CALL ME' 086 1803880 jigsaw.ie

- Irish Hospice Foundation (Bereavement) 1800 807077

If you find talking too hard. Drop a text or an email. This is the first step and you will be so glad you did. I am so proud of you!

"You can have flaws, be anxious, and even be angry, but do not forget that your life is the greatest enterprise in the world. Only you can stop it from going bust. Many appreciate you, admire you and love you.

Remember that to be happy is not to have a sky without a storm, a road without accidents, work without fatigue, relationships without disappointments.

To be happy is to find strength in forgiveness, hope in battles, security in the stage of fear, love in discord. It is not only to enjoy the smile, but also to reflect on the sadness. It is not only to celebrate the successes, but to learn lessons from the failures. It is not only to feel happy with the applause, but to be happy in anonymity.

Being happy is not a fatality of destiny, but an achievement for those who can travel within themselves. To be happy is to stop feeling like a victim and become your destiny's author. It is to cross deserts, yet to be able to find an oasis in the depths of our soul. It is to thank God for every morning, for the miracle of life.

Being happy is not being afraid of your own feelings. It's to be able to talk about you. It is having the courage to hear a "no". It is confidence in the face of criticism, even when unjustified. It is to kiss your children, pamper your parents, to live poetic moments with friends, even when they hurt us.

To be happy is to let live the creature that lives in each of us, free, joyful and simple.
It is to have maturity to be able to say: "I made mistakes".
It is to have the courage to say "I am sorry".
It is to have the sensitivity to say, "I need you".
It is to have the ability to say "I love you".

May your life become a garden of opportunities for happiness ...
That in spring may it be a lover of joy. In winter a lover of wisdom.
And when you make a mistake, start all over again.

For only then will you be in love with life. You will find that to be happy is not to have a perfect life. But use the tears to irrigate tolerance.

Use your losses to train patience.
Use your mistakes to sculptor serenity
Use pain to plaster pleasure.
Use obstacles to open windows of intelligence.

Never give up .... Never give up on people who love you. Never give up on happiness, for life is an incredible show."

Fernando Pessoa

Acknowledgements

To Aoife, thank you for everything you do. You have given me the love, encouragement and drive to finish this book. Thank you for showing me what love is again and for sticking with me through the tough days. Thank you for our baby boy, Eli. He makes me laugh and smile every single day without fail.

To Ava, Finn and Eli. You are all so amazing and I am such a proud father. I love you all so much.

To all my family and friends for helping me along my journey.

To Pat Divilly for his inspiration, his retreats and wonderful podcasts. A big thank you for telling me about the ManKind Project.

To the ManKind Project for allowing me to see my shadow and helping me understand myself. Thank you to all my fellow warriors for your courage, vulnerability and trust.

To Claire and Terry Lonergan for giving up their time to edit my book. They were both just amazing.

To all the people who have taught me huge life lessons and who have made me the strong person I am today.

To everyone single person who has helped me with my self-development over the last number of years.

Too many names to list. I hope I can help people in some way in the way you all have helped me.